THE ART OF DATING

The Art of Dating

THE ART OF DATING

BY EVELYN MILLIS DUVALL, PH.D.

with the collaboration of Joy Duvall Johnson

ASSOCIATION PRESS, NEW YORK

THE ART OF DATING

Copyright © *1958 by*
National Board of Young Men's Christian Associations

Association Press, 291 Broadway, New York 7, N. Y.

Second Printing, April, 1958

Library of Congress catalog card number: 58-6465

55

Printed in the United States of America
American Book–Stratford Press, Inc., New York

PREFACE

you = mad this

THIS BOOK is written for young people and the adults who care about them, as a guide to dating and the relationships between sexes.

When thousands of questions from youth were collected and analyzed as background for *Facts of Life and Love for Teen-Agers,* two of the most frequently asked questions were: (1) How do you get a date? and (2) What do you do with a date when you get one?

Since the publication of that book, I have continued to meet with young people in widely different settings—from the men at Princeton to the girls of the Indiana Sunshine Society; from Oberlin to South Carolina State; and with young people of both sexes in national and state-wide 4-H conventions, local and area YMCA, YWCA, and church youth groups, high school and college students, as well as out-of-school youth in many large and small communities in every section of the country.

In each instance, the most valuable part of our work together in discussing boy-girl relations was the full, frank, and free participation of the young people themselves. As they raised the questions they wanted to discuss and then consid-

v

ered them with me as consultant, much of value came to light.

Since 1950 more than 17,000 questions about dating have been collected from these sessions and analyzed for content as a basis for this book. Some thirty research studies, listed in the back of this volume, and a considerable amount of clinical evidence have been brought to bear upon the questions youth ask about dating. Where no specific data are available, the range of attitudes and opinions of youth themselves is incorporated with the general points of view that appear most frequently among them, their parents, teachers, and leaders.

Joy Duvall Johnson has collaborated in the preparation of this book from the initial content analysis of the mass of youth's questions to the actual writing and polishing of the material itself. As senior author, I assume responsibility for its content; at the same time I credit Joy for the faithfulness with which she reflects the point of view of youth, so close to her own generation.

This book, then, belongs to young people. It has come from them. It is directed to them. Our task as reporter and interpreter is done if the book serves not as a set of answers, but as a stimulus to further questioning; not as a directive, but as a guide. That is the spirit in which it was written.

EVELYN MILLIS DUVALL

CONTENTS

OFF TO A GOOD START

How?

Dating is one of the most exciting periods of your life. Suddenly, there are new horizons before you, friendships flower, your personality blooms, and your sense of being a desirable person worthy of affection becomes real. This is a time of great exhilaration, splendor, and discovery. To live it fully is to enjoy one of life's most delightful experiences.

To miss out on dating is a shame and a waste, especially when there is still time to do something about it. Dating is an art, and like all arts it must be cultivated to give results. Approach it with honesty, enthusiasm, energy, and it begins to take form. And soon you have answers to the questions that were worrying you.

Long before you actually start dating, you dream about it. Wistfully, you see other fellows and girls out together on dates, laughing, talking, going places, having a seemingly effortless, wonderful time. Before you ever get a date, you see yourself as the gallant hero or the glamorous heroine of a romantic situation. You imagine all the right words and actions so easily, so vividly, that you can hardly wait to start dating. Yet, somewhere inside you anticipate the awkward moments when you will stand tongue-tied and clumsy before some very special person, finding that dating is anything but wonderful. And so you swing between eagerness and anxiety, impatient to try your wings at one moment, and afraid of a take-off in the next.

When you consider the nature of dating, this emotional see-sawing is quite understandable. For dating fun is different from the fun a boy has playing ball with the fellows or the joy a girl knows confiding in her closest chum. In dating you are involved with persons of the other sex. You are learning about these other special people. And in the process you are also discovering a great deal about yourself. You are on the threshold of a new kind of experience that is grown-up, romantic, and full of promise for your life ahead as a full-fledged adult.

Probably you are wondering when you can start participating in this new exciting experience. For some of you the answer will be easy. If you belong to a closely knit group that does everything together, having dates within that circle of familiar friends will come naturally and simply. But for the majority of young people the answer is not so easy.

OVERCOMING BASHFULNESS

Shyness with members of the other sex is common among young people. You are not alone in this problem. Getting over self-consciousness to the point where you can relax and be friendly with those you most admire is a challenge. The more thrilled you are with the presence of the other person, the more likely you are to be embarrassed, it seems. But with experience you gradually become more comfortable with the opposite sex. Then, as you develop poise and self-confidence, you discover and put into practice more and more of the art of dating. How to develop that poise and confidence is the question.

Since girls grow up sooner, and are ready for dates before boys of their age and grade generally are, a particular problem for a teen-age girl is how to get a bashful boy to notice her. This is why girls' clubs so often center around planning boy-girl activities. Many a shy boy has come out of himself at a well-planned party. With encouragement he finds that he can carry on a conversation and have fun in a mixed group. Soon he, too, is ready for dates, usually first with the girl who was friendly and approachable while he was getting up his courage to ask her.

A fellow needs to be reasonably sure a girl wants to go out with him before he asks her. So it's a girl's responsibility to let a boy know that she is interested in him, without behaving so boldly that she scares him off.

When Girls Take the Initiative

There is a thin line between being available and being too forward. The girl who gets a reputation for being a flirt finds that many of the nicer boys and girls avoid her. Yet, when a girl acts too demure or feigns coolness or disinterest out of fear, she may chase boys away and miss out on the fun of friendship and dating. It is important to remember that boys are also scared and shy, and a smile or gesture from you can begin a friendship.

Girls frequently ask if it's all right to telephone the boys they like. Well—let's look at it from the boy's point of view. If Joan calls Bill about a specific question, or to invite him to some definite affair, he can respond without necessarily feeling that she has put him on the spot. If she calls repeatedly, or for no particular purpose except to chat aimlessly, his family may tease him and he becomes embarrassed by her "chasing."

Custom has it that a girl may speak first when meeting a boy on the street or in the hallway at school. She doesn't have to wait for the boy to nod or address her. It's simple courtesy that she recognize him with some friendly greeting or gesture. She does this by making some pleasant sign that she recognizes the boy, and that she feels friendly toward him. She may smile or nod, or say "Hello" or "Hi, Bill!" Perhaps she'll add some casual remark.

But a girl should not interrupt a boy who is talking to someone or is with a group of fellows, or is obviously absorbed in something else. That, too, is simple courtesy. If a boy indicates his awareness of her by disengaging himself from the group, or shows her in some other way that he knows she's there, she greets him.

A girl gets a reputation for being "fast" not because she's friendly toward boys but because of the way she behaves when they are around. The "forward" girl overly emphasizes the fact that she's a female——by the way in which she dresses, walks, talks, looks, and laughs. She goes beyond the bounds of what is considered "nice" in her attention to the boys. By her seductiveness she encourages boys to be too fresh, too loud, and too boisterous.

Is it ever all right for a girl to chase a boy? Throughout the ages women have found ways of being appealing and interesting to the men they have liked. Nowadays girls are taking more initiative than ever. The important thing is that a girl not be too obvious, or she defeats her own purpose. It's best if she waits for some sign of a boy's interest before she embarks on a campaign. And then she must make it look as though he, rather than she, is the pursuer. In Grandma's formula, it's all right for a girl to "chase a fellow until he catches her."

BOY MEETS GIRL

How does a fellow get to meet a girl he likes? is a question many boys ask. Girls who have to use subtle approaches think a boy has no real problem in this direction. But what a boy really wants to know is how to operate so that his advances won't be rebuffed.

Traditionally, a boy asks a mutual acquaintance to introduce him to a girl he wants to meet. He takes it from there, usually with an invitation to a date that will further their acquaintance.

In modern settings it's not always easy to find a go-between. Fortunately, today it's no longer necessary. If a boy and girl attend the same school or classes, or belong to the same club, that in itself constitutes an introduction. If Janet goes to a different school, then Ted can try attending one or more of her school's functions in an effort to meet her.

The hardest moment, perhaps, comes when a couple are finally face to face. If a boy is an outgoing type of person to whom friendly pleasantries come easily, then it's easy. He'll find the right little compliment to pay a girl, the right opening remarks. But the shy, inexperienced boy—and he is legion—will find these first efforts at gallantry very trying. Such a boy ought to plan ahead of time just what he will say to a girl. Even then he may not follow through with his plan; tension may erase every rehearsed word from his mind and he may end up blurting out an abrupt invitation that startles the girl. But if she is sensitive and interested, she overlooks his clumsiness and encourages him with her acceptance, knowing that experience will take the rough edges off her new friend's manner.

Meeting a strange girl in a strange place can really give a boy stage fright. This time he had no chance to rehearse; suddenly he's expected to do and say the right things. It's no wonder that he gets tongue-tied. (Of course, later on, in long solitary post-mortems, he can think of the most brilliant, most witty conversation.) That's why it's a good idea for beginning daters to develop a few little formulas to use when words fail.

A good opener, for instance, would be: "Didn't I meet you at the Joneses?" Or a boy might make a comment that linked them to a common friend or interest. He could also ask a girl where she hails from, what brought her to this place, how she spells her name, or how long she has known the person who introduced them. Such simple little icebreakers that get conversation rolling are worth developing.

All Work and No Play

Many high school and college girls complain that the boys they know have no time for girls. And it is true that there are serious-minded boys of all ages who are so absorbed in school work, hobbies, or plans for the future that they pay little or no attention to girls. A fellow with his mind on the future, busily weighing the pros and cons of business versus the professions, considering whether college or military training should come first, seemingly cannot further complicate his life with a girl. And before he knows it he has a reputation as a "woman hater."

There are young men so absorbed in work or study that they can talk about nothing else. Girls complain that such a man is a bore—that he never seems to notice them or their interests, that he's unwilling to do anything to cultivate a friendship. This kind of self-absorbed boy who is essentially nice often misses out on the friendship of a suitable girl and then falls prey to an unscrupulous one who plays upon his central interest to make an insincere place for herself in his life.

Some boys and girls who appear to be devoted to an absorbing interest actually are afraid of members of the other sex, and use their interest as an excuse to avoid contact with them. A girl who doesn't want to be too obvious in her datelessness may feign busyness or an intense interest in music or her family, for instance, to cover up for her lack of boy friends. Similarly, a boy's interest in planes, electronics, sports, or what-have-you may, in reality, be masking his fear of being unable to win and hold a girl's attention. Such boys and girls would do well to face up to the truth, and, with the help of a wise counselor or good friend, change their ways to catch up on some wholesome dating fun.

Some young people have intellectual, aesthetic, or spiritual interests during high school which are just enough out of step with the majority of their age and grade so that they don't find their associates congenial until they get into college or university life. These are the fellows and girls whose abilities seem to overshadow their personalities in their early development. They "come out" as interesting persons as they find themselves, but as teens they are discouraging both to themselves and to those who care about them. The important thing to remember is that social development and maturity cannot be rushed, and that eventually most young people find their proper social niche.

Not Ready to Date?

It's a good idea to investigate the reason why a particular individual is slow to get started dating. Is he shy and bashful? Then maybe he needs encouragement in getting social experience; maybe he or she needs to be drawn into a group activity as a starter.

Is the person an outsider because of interests and dreams that are not shared by his contemporaries? Then he needs further to develop his unique personality, confident that congenial companions will be available beyond high school or even college.

Some young people have been so hurt in the process of growing up that they may need special help to straighten out. They must be made to realize that they have within them the potentialities of becoming wholesome, happy persons. Special counselors, psychological services, and guidance facilities can help this kind of unhappy young person; and those who are concerned with his happiness should carefully guide him in that direction.

Too Ready to Date?

Frequently girls are ready for dates long before others of their age and grade are. These are the girls who grow up fast, and before they're out of grade school  are taller or more physically mature than others in their class. They become interested in boys at a time when fellows their own age are not even aware that girls exist, in a special personal sense.

Because the early developing girl is tall for her age, it is hard for her to find a boy taller than she is and still within the range of those considered datable by her family. Parents often object to a girl's dating older boys, for they know that although she looks grown-up, she actually is too inexperienced to handle the complicated situations that might arise with an older fellow. Yet the boys of her own age are still "little guys" both literally and socially. So the early maturing girl is expected to "freeze" where she is until others of her age catch up with her.

The fact is that at junior high school age, girls are taller than the majority of boys. Lamentably, at dancing classes, group dates, or boy-girl parties, the tall girl who is big for her age is avoided by shorter fellows. So she, more ready to date than most, is most frequently delayed in the very social experiences, such as dancing lessons, that would ready her for dating when it finally does come. This problem is accentuated in our country because exaggerated emphasis is put on the importance of a boy being taller than a girl.

There are some particularly well-adjusted girls who weather this handicap quite nicely. They become natural leaders to whom other girls and boys turn. They take the initiative in social affairs and help others have a good time. By the time pairing off begins, and the fellows are beginning to shoot up in height, such early maturing girls come into their own. Their chances are especially good if they have in the meantime developed some special skills in group activities, such as running a party or playing a musical instrument, or have found themselves a place in sports or drama.

HOW TO BE POPULAR

Most teen-agers would like to be popular if they could. But many are baffled as to just what it takes to achieve popularity, or even to get a date. Knowing what is generally considered attractive to the opposite sex helps. Also understanding what boys expect of girls and what girls expect of boys in a given community is especially important.

In general, young people like members of the other sex who are (1) careful of their personal appearance; (2) courteous and thoughtful; and (3) fun to be with.

A girl doesn't have to be a beauty to get a date. She just has to dress appropriately, be neat and well groomed, and then try to forget her appearance. The same goes for a boy. If he's clean and neat (hair combed, fresh shirt, nails clean) he's acceptable, and probably attractive to someone.

Courtesy is mentioned frequently by both boys and girls as a desirable quality in a date. Actually, being courteous is just being thoughtful of others; it's easy to get the habit. Sometimes a young person grows up in a family that is careless or casual about little courtesies, and he has to learn not to speak when someone else is talking, not to talk with a mouth full of food. If you keep your voice low and pleasant, say "Thank you" and "Excuse me" at appropriate times, it makes a pleasant impression on new and old friends. Some schools have special courses in social arts where students get opportunities for practicing those graces that make getting along with others easy. Books, articles, and lectures also help to give boys and girls an idea of what kind of behavior is expected of them when they begin to have dates.

When you say "Ted is such fun to be with!" do you know why? Do you realize it takes practice to become a "fun person"? It involves some rather complicated skills—knowing how to carry on a conversation, knowing how to enter a group pleasantly, being able to accept and refuse invitations graciously, assuming responsibility for one's part in the group activity, and generally making others glad that you're there. Most boys and girls are awkward in group situations at first. But as they gain experience, first in simple situations with others who know and like them, they get over being self-conscious. Soon they become so poised that they feel at home in most social situations. But this takes time and experience—lots of it.

It is no accident that boys and girls who have belonged to clubs and organizations get along more easily with people than do those who have grown up somewhat isolated. Being a member of a group not only gives you experience in planning and making decisions with others, in carrying responsibility for your part in a project, but it also introduces you to a variety of human situations and human beings. You begin to learn how the next guy "ticks."

If you want to be more acceptable to the other sex, then you ought to get into group activities with other young people of both sexes. Mingling with a mixed group will ready you for dating and develop those skills which will help you carry off a date successfully.

THE DATE FOR YOU

It's common knowledge that certain teen-age girls swoon over movie and TV stars. There was Elvis Presley, for instance, and before him Frank Sinatra, and long before his time Rudolph Valentino. But few girls actually ever expect to date such an idol. In fact, one of the functions of the celebrity is to serve as a focus for early infatuation without ever requiring the girl to do anything about it. It's just as common for a fellow to daydream about a movie queen—and a good safe practice, because he will never be expected to court and win her.

Occasionally, however, a young person goes overboard in a crush on some unattainable person, so that he doesn't make progress with those who are realistically available to him. It's not just the movie or TV personality who's unattainable. Many a young girl swoons over the football captain, the president of the senior class, or the most popular boy in the school, with whom she hasn't the ghost of a chance. Indeed, she wouldn't even know what to do on such a spectacular date if she had it. Similarly, an inexperienced boy will sometimes moon over a popular teacher, or the school queen—as unattainable for him as Miss Universe.

As long as these superromantic crushes prevail, the inexperienced boy or girl will probably make little progress in getting a date with anyone; for no real and available person can rival the "dream's" charms and popularity.

Realistically, the beginning dater starts with someone who is not much more socially active than he is. The boy who has never dated courts rejection or failure by asking out the most popular girl in the class two years ahead of him. But he may make a good start with a friendly not-too-experienced girl a year or two younger than he is. A girl who wants to begin dating should look about for some pleasant, shy, interested fellow in her own grade (or a class or so beyond) rather than wistfully pine for an older, inaccessible man about town.

PROVE IT TO YOUR PARENTS

Many a girl comes home with stars in her eyes at having been asked out by a boy, only to find her parents objecting on the grounds that she is still too young to date. And often a boy wants to take a girl out, but his mother or father insists that he give his full attention to his studies, saying, "There's plenty of time later for playing around with girls."

How can parents be convinced that you are ready for dates? This is a question that is asked by young people all over the country. Sometimes, of course, the parents are right, and their son or daughter is too immature to date. Actually it is up to you to prove that you're ready to go out by proving that you're grown-up. How do you do that? By taking real responsibility around the house; by helping with chores such as car-washing, cleaning, lawn-mowing, by showing an understanding and concern for your family's problems and budget, by doing your school job well.

Maybe you'll also have to help your parents understand current dating habits in your community, so that they develop confidence in the social situations open to teen-agers. It helps to encourage mothers and fathers to get out to parents' meetings, to attend neighborhood affairs, and to keep up to date on school and social events. This last is *your* job. Do you let your folks in on your activities?

WHY NOT TALK ABOUT IT?

Many adults, and some young people too, frequently ask if reading books on dating and talking about dating problems actually help. There's no question about it—the more you learn about dating, the better. The fear that such guidance will "give young people ideas beyond their years" is groundless. Actually, if they did not have the ideas, they wouldn't find such reading of interest. Getting perspective on how other people feel, finding out what is generally expected of you on a date, becoming aware of the many ways you can approach the problem of getting along with others, and coming to terms with your unique answer to life's questions about men and women—all are facilitated by good reading and good discussions of dating, love, and marriage.

Furthermore, books about dating usually point up the fact that all the haunting questions, confusions, and problems that so baffle and hurt are common to most young people. It's encouraging to know that one is not alone—that others are shy, others are clumsy. Reading from a printed page about a poignant experience that you thought was yours alone lessens your sense of loneliness and isolation, makes you feel close to others again.

Of course, there is literature designed to be sexually stimulating rather than thought-provoking. Some jokes and talk are sexy and cheap too. But it's easy to differentiate. That discussion is worth-while if it aims at "growing you up" into the kind of person you want to become. You'll usually find it with other like-minded people, under a wise leader, in school, church group, or informal club, or even among close friends who bring out the best in each other.

2

ARE YOU READY TO DATE?

How is it that some people start dating at such a young age, and others are so much older before they begin to have dates? Both teen-agers and their parents often wonder what is the best age to begin dating. The question looms even more nowadays because so many young people start their dating so early in life. Should parents be concerned? Is there really a special age at which dating should begin?

WHEN TEEN-AGERS START DATING

The Purdue Opinion Panel Poll of high school students reported in 1957 that 31 per cent of the boys and 40 per cent of the girls started to date before they were fourteen years old. This means that a good many teen-agers begin to date before they get into high school. It also confirms the observation that girls, in general, tend to mature earlier and start dating earlier than boys, age for age.

But still another finding of the Purdue Poll of 10th, 11th, and 12th grade high school students is that one out of eight teen-agers doesn't date at all! How come that some young people start having dates even before they're in high school, and others have no dating experience whatsoever during their teens? What do teen-agers themselves have to say on this subject?

THE TEENS TALK...

When thousands of representative high school students were asked the question, "At what age do you think teen-agers should have their first date?" 41 per cent answered thirteen to fourteen, and 46 per cent said fifteen to sixteen. Such replies indicate that most students feel that the first date should occur in the middle or early teens. It also suggests that many teen-agers appear to date earlier than they really think they should. Why? Who is it that starts dating earliest?

The Early Bird

The Purdue University survey found that high school students living in the western part of the United States start dating at earlier ages than do southern young people (47 per cent of those in the West as compared with 34 per cent of the southerners). Even more interesting is the finding that young people from the higher socioeconomic groups start dating at younger ages than do those from either the middle-income or the lower-income groups.

WHY SOME DATE EARLIER THAN OTHERS

There are interlocking reasons why some teen-agers start having dates at earlier ages than do others. Such factors as these are all interrelated: (1) how their parents feel about early dating; (2) how ready the boy or girl is for dating; (3) how much social experience a young person has had; and (4) how many social opportunities there are open to a given age and social set.

The Folks at Home

Parents who are socially active themselves tend to encourage their sons and daughters to participate in social events from early ages. They arrange mixed parties for their children, send them to dancing classes, buy them the proper clothes for various occasions, and in every way they can, urge them into social situations. The Purdue Poll finding that dating starts earlier in higher socioeconomic groups is understandable. Young people whose parents are socially active have the opportunity to socialize freely from childhood onward. They are acquainted with the children of their parents' friends long before they reach their teens. They are involved with neighbors, church, and community activities. Their parents expect this—they urge their children into the social life of the community so that they will eventually take their place in their social circles.

Ambitious middle-class parents more often want their sons and daughters to pay attention to school work and vocational goals before they get distracted by dating. Families with a different socioeconomic background and outlook, on the other hand, expect their children to get jobs as soon as they can and help out at home even before school graduation.

So it is easy to see how such widely different dating habits exist. Some teen-agers are pressured into dates early by their families, and others are pressured by parents into postponing dates as long as possible.

At Your Own Pace

Of course, some teen-agers are ready for dates before others are. They simply mature earlier. The boy who shoots up tall and manly in his early teens is ready for dates before the "shorty" in his class. The girl who develops early so that she fills a strapless evening gown gracefully is datable at a time when her schoolmates are still looking and behaving like little girls.

The late-maturing boy or girl is just not as interested in the other sex and consequently not as interesting as a dating partner either. But the time will come when the slower-developing youngsters of both sexes catch up. Such a "late-bloomer" should be reassured that there is nothing wrong with maturing late. In fact, there are advantages. The girl who doesn't go "boy-crazy" has opportunities to develop lasting intellectual and cultural interests, to make close friends among other girls, to excel in some skill or art. Certainly the late-maturing youngster need not feel "queer." For a boy, this "breathing spell" between childhood and manhood is an opportunity to get a good start on vocational training, to develop meaningful hobbies, and even to enjoy his family more than is possible for the precocious lad who spends so much of his time and energy on dates. Even so, the late-maturing girl or boy may feel out of things for a while simply because he or she is not personally ready for dates yet.

EXPERIENCE COUNTS

The young person who has belonged to social groups since he was a child slips into dating situations more easily during adolescence than does the youngster who was not socially active as a child. Why? Because he has developed social skills that the less experienced youngster has yet to learn. He knows how to carry on a conversation, how to handle an introduction, how to dance, how to eat properly, how to accept and to refuse an invitation. All these and many other social skills are learned in action with other people.

Some boys and girls pick up the normal courtesies and social behaviors as a matter of course during their childhood. They are fortunate—and don't suffer the embarrassment that confronts teen-agers who have not had such opportunities.

The young person with limited social experience must tackle the tasks of becoming socially comfortable with other people in a variety of situations as he approaches dating age. This is not always easy, but it must be done before he can feel at ease in dating situations.

It's Up to You

Occasionally one finds a young person who bitterly blames his lack of social success on his background. He feels that be-

cause he grew up on the wrong side of the tracks or in a lower-income family, he is behind the eight ball. This kind of attitude is self-defeating and unfortunate. It's not confined to teen-agers either, but is common among those of every age who waste energy complaining about their lack of advantages, rather than using it to improve their lot.

Vernon is the kind of fellow who might have been licked by his background. His family lived in a shabby house in the poorest part of town. His father was hardly the kind of man of whom any boy could be proud, and his mother was little better. Vernon never was allowed to invite friends to his home, and he had to forego belonging to clubs and organizations in order to work and help support his family. But Vernon wouldn't let circumstances defeat him. His gay spirit and wit and his talent for telling a good story took him into many a group as he became older. And his sympathy for the underdog, his concern for the underprivileged, won him a place in one after another project from grammar school onward. Like many of the world's great men, he made stumbling blocks into stepping stones and rose above his handicaps.

Any young person has the answer to his social problems within himself. When he really wants to, he can grow in his ability to win friends and acceptance. Often the person who has to forge a place for himself develops a special charm that more privileged individuals lack. A person's true individuality is his own to develop—in his own way and at his own pace throughout life.

WHAT ARE THE CHANCES?

Do you have a real opportunity for dating? This is the key factor which determines when you begin to date. If you have no one to go with, then you can't date, no matter how ready you are. If there are few social events in your school or community attended by both boys and girls, your dating may again be delayed—that is, unless you take matters into your own hands. Creating opportunities of your own may be hazardous, or it may make the difference between dating or not dating at all. So let's look at some of the factors involved.

Offered—Friends and Fun

Some schools, churches, and communities provide plenty of opportunities for young people to date and become socially expert. They offer a good youth program in which any young

person can find friends and activities, and they encourage wholesome interrelationships between the sexes.

When the social program is combined with opportunities for discussing and reviewing one's personal progress, young people have a real advantage. During the teen years, and on into young adulthood, most persons of both sexes are striving to find themselves, to become accepted as persons as well as dating partners. They need to know not only what is expected of them on a date, but how to develop into attractive and interesting men and women.

Schools, churches, and youth-serving agencies provide many-faceted programs in which young people can find themselves and their interests—and share those interests. Often they themselves help initiate social boy-girl programs as well as informal and regular courses that prepare for wholesome dating experiences.

"A Stranger in Town"

Sometimes a young person finds himself in a strange town where he knows few, if any, datable young people. Perhaps he has transferred to a new school or this is his first year away at college. The question is—how to make the friends that lead to dating?

It's natural for a girl or boy in a new place to feel insecure among strangers. "Will they like me?" "What do they expect of me here as a person?" "How can I get to know the people I'll like and who will like me?" These and many other questions keep arising.

A teen-ager in such a situation may avoid new people just because he's afraid of making a wrong impression. The result then is that others may think of him as a snob and avoid him. How much better to do something *positive* to get into the swing of things! A boy or girl in a strange new school could join a club, get a spot on the school paper, try out for the glee club, the drama group, the hockey team, or get on a committee. Just telling the school counselor or home room teacher of your eagerness to get into activities is a good start. Once the ice is broken, the rest is relatively easy.

School Ties

Possibly your dating experience is hampered by the fact that you are attending an all-boys' or all-girls' school. Then it's necessary to date people from other schools if you date at all. Your school may plan mixed parties with another school.

Young people that you meet at such functions will probably be suitable as dates.

Going out with students from other schools can be fun—if it's not overdone. Dating people outside your school to the exclusion of the boys and girls in your class is a mistake. As a teen-ager you need to be in with a group who has similar interests and is near enough for a Coke and chatter after school.

A Word to the Wise

Most teen-agers stick pretty well within one group for their dates and parties. Occasionally, however, you may be invited to a party where some of the guests are strangers to you. Suppose, while you're there, you meet a boy who seems nice and who wants to take you home. How will you know if he's a suitable escort? There are some things you may want to consider before giving him your answer.

You might ask the adult in charge of the party about the boy and his reputation. Or you might speak with the hostess. If these people speak well of the fellow, you could accept his invitation. But first make sure that he hasn't brought another girl to the party, whom he is planning to ditch. You don't want to be the cause of someone else's discomfort.

If there *is* some question about the boy's reputation, or if no one at the party knows him well enough to say, the safest thing is to stay out of the situation. If you'd like to get to know him better, you might suggest that another couple whom you know well join you in riding home. If no one else is going your way, you can politely refuse this time, and invite him to your house some afternoon to meet your parents and listen to records. As you get to know him better, you'll learn whether or not he's the kind of person you'd like to date.

BLIND DATING

Blind dating is a legitimate way to meet people, but there are a few things to consider before you go into it. First of all, who is making the arrangements? How well do you know this person? How responsible is he or she? How much does he know about your prospective dating partner?

If there is any uncertainty about the blind date, it may be best to decline with thanks or suggest some safe dating situation. You might, for instance, suggest an informal party with several other couples you know. Perhaps your church group is having an outing to which the blind date might be invited as your guest. In blind dating, a good principle is: Take advantage of opportunities, but provide safeguards.

Off Limits

If you're going out with a boy or girl whom you don't know well, it's best to avoid public places the first time. In fact, even if you know your date well, some public places are just not suitable for young people. Many public dance halls, for instance, draw an unscrupulous crowd of people who could cause a difficult situation for you and your date. Bars and roadside taverns have people in them occasionally who might cause trouble. Roaming the streets with or without an escort is risky in certain parts of town.

Likewise, people you meet in public places are rarely suitable dating prospects. Those boys sitting behind you and your girl friends in the movies might quite possibly be nice, but they might also turn out to be roughnecks. It's much better to ignore them than to take a chance. The boy who cuts in at a community dance may look cute, but he might be more than you can handle if you let him take you home without finding out about him first. As a general rule, it's safer to stay with people you know or have met through suitable channels.

Pickups

Pickups are risky. It may seem adventurous to stand on a corner and pick up a likely-looking person, but it can be dangerous. The papers are filled with unhappy, sometimes tragic, incidents of teen-agers who took such wild chances. People who use the pickup system are those who for some reason cannot use the ordinary channels for meeting people.

Boys sometimes congregate on corners to whistle at passing girls. It may feel good to be whistled at, but unless you know the boys, it's not wise to encourage them. Many fellows feel that an easy pickup is "fast," or else she wouldn't be out looking for a date in that fashion.

This is not just a matter of concern to girls. Boys too can be exploited by unscrupulous women whom they pick up. There are less risky ways of getting dates than picking them up on street corners.

Safe and Sane

If you want a safe place to meet people—and a place that promises wholesome fun—first look toward your church. Many churches have young people's programs with activities designed to help you make and keep friends of both sexes. People you meet in a church group are generally the kind who are responsible and respectable.

Community centers, YMCAs, YWCAs, USOs, and neighborhood clubs provide all kinds of interesting programs for teen-agers and young adults. If you want more friends, explore some of your local resources and before you know it you'll be deep in activity.

FOLLOW YOUR INTERESTS

The key to the whole question of finding suitable dating partners lies within yourself. If you're interested in acting, you'll find the kind of date you would enjoy more quickly by joining a dramatic club or class than by hanging around the locker rooms at school. Not only that—but you and this new friend would have a common interest from the very first, which would help overcome the initial problem of what to say to your date.

If there is no dramatic club in your vicinity you might start a little play-acting group. Invite some of your friends who also like to act for the purpose of creating a skit for a school or church meeting.

If you like to sing or play a musical instrument, the school or local community choral group or band would be a good place to meet eligible dating partners with similar interests.

Somewhere there is a group or organization that will fit *your* interests and provide datable companions.

SUMMING UP

There's no one age at which anyone is old enough to have dates. In general, young people today date at an earlier age than did their own parents. Girls usually begin to have dates at an earlier age than do boys. Some young people of both sexes start dating in junior high school, or even earlier, while others are out of senior high school before they really begin to have dates. Some parents urge their sons and daughters to mingle with others of their age and to go out with mixed groups from the time they're children. Other parents reluctantly permit their young people to have dates even when they are well into their teens. These and many other factors make a difference in the age at which any particular person begins to date.

You're old enough to have dates when you're mature enough to assume responsibility for your dating behavior, when you have learned enough social poise to get and keep a date, and when you have convinced your parents and others interested in you of your readiness for these special boy-girl experiences.

The age at which you start to date is not as important as is how you behave when you do begin. Popularity as a goal in itself is empty, and dating at any cost is self-defeating. The boy or girl who starts out with an exploitive, cheap, sexy, blind-alley kind of approach may be seriously hurt and handicapped in the long run. The young person who starts with real interest in others and with eagerness to cultivate sincere friendships is on the happy road to satisfying relationships with boys and girls, men and women, through the years ahead.

WHAT ABOUT YOUR DATE'S AGE?

Parents and other adults tend to prefer that young people date within their own age group. It's usual for high school students to be encouraged to date within their own class, where there is little age difference between boy and girl. Even in college many social events are held on the assumption that coeds will attend with boys from their own class.

OLDER THAN HIS GIRL

When you get down to cases, you find that more often than not the boy is a little older than the girl he takes out. There are several very good reasons for this trend. First is the fact that girls tend to mature before boys of their own age and are ready for dates a couple of years earlier. Secondly, because of the difference in the rate of their development, a girl often has more in common with a slightly older boy than with a lad of her own age. Thirdly, a boy often feels more secure with a younger girl than with one who is superior in status and experience. Then again, some parents prefer their daughters to date somewhat older boys who are supposed to be more mature and responsible.

This early difference in dating age between boys and girls continues throughout life generally. The tendency is for girls to date boys a couple of years older than they, and for women to marry men who are their elders by a year or two or more. This doesn't mean that a man ought to be older; it just means that he usually is.

Differences—within Reason

The usual difference in age between a girl and the fellow she dates is one to two years. Dating someone fairly close to your own age has several advantages. You're both at about the same stage of life and generally interested in the same things. You both know the same people and move in a social group with other people of your own age. Also important, although not as generally recognized, is that public opinion tends to favor your dating someone of approximately your own age. Let a girl date a much older fellow and her parents protest, her friends wonder, her neighbors gossip. If she dates a fellow of about her own age, friends and family usually approve.

Just how much difference in age is acceptable is hard to determine definitely, because individual cases differ so much. A girl of fourteen or sixteen may be quite mature for her age and have more in common with a senior boy than with someone in her own grade. A boy may be relatively inexperienced socially and therefore feel more comfortable with a girl two or three years younger than himself. But usually, one, two, or three years difference in age is accepted. When greater differences occur, further questions are relevant.

The Much Older Fellow

Often very young girls, who are just beginning to think about dates, yearn to go out with "older men." Looking around, they see most of the boys in their own grade absorbed in baseball, model planes, and other "kid stuff." Then they see seventeen- and eighteen-year-old seniors driving cars, taking girls out gallantly, providing all the excitement they yearn for. They themselves are shy and self-conscious in social situations, but the senior boy is poised, sure of himself. He's also in the midst of a social swing, while they're on the lonely fringes. So it's understandable that many a younger girl longs for a chance to date with a poised, popular, older boy.

The same thing occurs at the college level; freshman girls pine for the attentions of the sophisticated upperclassmen. The senior man strides across the campus apparently self-assured; he belongs to the charmed inner circle of those who rate. Pity the poor self-conscious freshman lad who has to compete with this older man-about-campus in getting dates!

Sometimes, though rarely, a much younger girl does get that coveted date with an older boy. When it does happen, there are hazards. The older boy who "robs the cradle" may not be as popular among his own age group as he appears to be. He may really feel so insecure that he has to date a considerably younger girl to cover his uneasiness. Sometimes he asks a younger girl out because she appears to be more easily exploited.

Hook, Line, and Sinker

There is some evidence to support the fear that when an older male seeks the company of a young girl, it's just because she's innocent and easily exploited. Girls of his own age and social experience have, by this time, learned to protect themselves from unwelcome advances. They have become skillful in avoiding potentially hazardous situations and in warding off invitations that they don't wish to accept.

The young, unaware girl lacks these techniques which come with social experience, and so appears to be "easy" to the older, exploitive male. She has not been around enough yet to know what is and what is not expected of her. She fears that she will get a reputation as a "prude" or "chicken" if she refuses to go along with her date's suggestions. She doesn't want to offend this superior male—so much older, smoother, and supposedly wiser. She can't differentiate sincerity from "a line," and fails to perceive or stop the sequence of events that leads into situations she can't handle.

"Sweet talk" flatters the young girl. She really believes that he has never seen eyes like hers, nor smelled hair so sweet.

She wants so much to be loved that she accepts at face value his declaration of love at first sight. She delights in his excessive attentions, not realizing that they're the age-old ways in which a man paves the way for intimacies. But then, when he begins to be urgent in his demands, she is offended, bewildered, and frightened. This happens, of course, because she has not recognized the step-by-step process and so is unprepared for the end result.

A fellow is often baffled by such behavior in a girl. He asks quite bluntly, "Why is it that a nice girl will lead you on and then not be willing to go through with it?" What he fails to see is that what is obvious to him as a male is not at all clear to a young, inexperienced girl. He knows the meaning of a sex-toned situation. He is aware of sexual excitation from its beginning. But the young female has no such clear-cut sensations. She reacts to the earlier stages of love play with relaxation and enjoyment at being cuddled. It's not until the man becomes "fresh" that she's aware of what is happening.

Not all older fellows date young girls with the purpose of seduction. Sometimes an older boy may have been preoccupied with work or studies while others of his age were dating. When he does start going out with girls he finds that he's more comfortable with younger girls who are at his own level of social poise. Also many an older fellow is genuinely interested in and charmed by a young girl; he would be shocked to learn that adults are assuming that he wants only to exploit her.

Lester is a case in point. He was a studious lad all through high school, entering into few activities outside his studies and basketball. In college he made the basketball team and got straight A's in his courses. He loved to read and devoted a lot of time to that. From college he went on to a seminary where his studies and student preaching took up all his time.

By the time he was ordained he was twenty-six and ready to get married. But now he found that the young women his own age were either married or so socially aggressive that they frightened him. As a result he started going out with a junior in college who shared his intellectual interests and encouraged him into the social life he had missed. The relationship was hardly exploitive—but mutually helpful—and ended, upon the girl's graduation, in a happy marriage.

It's clear, then, that age is only one factor. While there are some boys and men who date much younger girls for the advantage it gives them in "the battle of the sexes," this is not always the case by any means. One has to know the persons involved to predict the dangers and rewards that their relationship may reap.

It All Depends . . .

A point frequently discussed in high school is whether it's advisable for a high school girl to date a college man. In general, high school boys tend to oppose the practice vigorously as unfair and unwise. The girls are not quite so positive. They argue that dating a college boy gives a girl real prestige among other girls. It introduces her to college functions and to other college students of both sexes. It makes her feel grown-up, and not infrequently leads to her getting pinned and engaged much sooner than if she had restricted her dates to high school boys.

The other side of the argument recognizes that a girl who dates college boys may be cutting off her chances to date the boys in her own school. She may miss out on the normal social life of the school. She may not find a real sense of belonging with the college set, in whose interests and conversation she cannot participate fully. And she may also find that the college man who takes out a high school girl expects to be rewarded by favors that the college girls do not generally permit.

In the last analysis, what really must be considered are the personalities of the college boy and the high school girl involved. If they have a great deal in common and find delight in sharing a multitude of similar interests; if he enjoys the hospitality of her home, while she thrills to occasional campus affairs—they may both feel that these advantages outweigh those of being cut off from their own classmates.

Whether a girl dates a college boy or not, she should be aware of the gains and losses incurred by her actions. This will make a choice easier and safeguard both her and the boy from unrewarding situations.

DATING OUT-OF-SCHOOL FELLOWS

Both high school and college girls meet the question of whether to accept a date with an out-of-school fellow. What is important to remember is that by dropping out of school a boy limits his vocational and social future. The fellow who finishes his education and establishes himself in a profession or business does better through the years than does the boy who drops out of school. Recent figures show that the lifetime earnings of a high school graduate total on the average some $165,000, while the lifetime earnings of a college graduate average about $268,000—over $100,000 more! The same census report indicates that the more education a person has, the better his prospects for future earnings. Of course, there are some exceptional boys who drop out and still do well, but by and large there is a close connection between schooling and level of income.

Nowadays almost any boy may continue on in school if he wants to badly enough. Dropping out of school usually indicates a lack of ambition. Or it reveals that a fellow takes a dim view of himself and his potentialities. Sometimes the pressure of his home may make a boy drop out. More boys from poor homes stop school than do middle- or upper-class fellows. They get jobs to help out at home—and then marry soon afterward. Therefore, one of the factors that enters into dating a "drop-out" is not only the possible difference in age, but sometimes even more important, the difference in social expectations and status and in the style of life that each represents. Such differences need not be but can be serious in both dating and in marriage.

Of course, an out-of-school man may already have completed his education, be vocationally established, and ready to settle down in a home of his own. In such a case, a girl would be dating and eventually marrying a man of her own social and economic level.

Elsie Jackson, for instance, taught school for several years after her graduation from the School of Education at the state university. When she began to date Ralph, he was about her age, having graduated from the School of Business the same year she had. After graduation he went into business with his father. Last year Ralph's dad died and left him the entire firm. In dating each other, Elsie and Ralph found that they had much in common, that each dreamed of the same kind of future, the same way of life. It was no surprise to their friends when after a year and a half of steady dating they married and settled down in the community that was home to them both.

Quite a different situation exists with Martha and Paul. Martha is a junior in high school who has gone out several times with Paul. At twenty-six, Paul is still unmarried, and running his father's hotel on the main street of town. Paul is ready for marriage. He needs a woman in his life, and to help him with his work at the hotel. Martha, on the other hand, is gay and spirited, full of fun, and not yet ready for the kind of settled life Paul desires. Martha's parents are relieved to find that she now senses what they feared from the beginning. Thrilling as it is to have Paul's love and proposal of marriage, Martha is in the tough position of having to marry him very soon or break off completely with him; for, being older, out of school and eager to get married, he is impatient with a schoolgirl's reluctance to settle down. He doesn't want to play around with the younger set as she does. A person like Elsie might find in Paul the same kind of stability she enjoys in her Ralph, but for Martha, Paul is far too urgent and mature for either marriage or dating.

In dating older out-of-school men, then, one of the key questions is how ready the girl is for marriage and how willing she is to give up her own way of life for the settled one of a mature man.

"MY WIFE DOESN'T UNDERSTAND ME . . ."

There should be no question about it—in dating a married man a girl always takes a risk. Such a man is not free to take a girl out, to make love to her, or to marry her. Until he is free, he is expected to consort only with his wife, and to engage in social activities where there is no pairing off with other women. Many a lonely married man seeks the companionship of an understanding woman. If she's young, she brings him the added sensation of feeling youthful again himself. If she is sympathetic, she may meet deep emotional needs within him. He, on the other hand, may appear to her to be seasoned, wise, mature, experienced. She may feel flattered by his attention. She may be touched by confessions of how his wife misunderstands him. And before she knows it, she's involved beyond her expectations in mixed emotions that lead all too often to heartache.

Sometimes a girl walks into such a relationship with her eyes wide open. More often, though, the man doesn't tell the girl he's married, for fear she won't date him. And usually the relationship has progressed some distance before the girl

is aware of the actual situation. By that time she may be too fond of the man or too sorry for him to know how to withdraw effectively. The wisest thing, of course, is for a girl to break off a relationship as soon as she discovers that a man is married.

If she can uncover his matrimonial status before she ever goes out with him, she is on still safer ground. This isn't always easy, especially in relationships that spring up without proper sponsorship. If a girl meets a man through a friend or member of the family, she can learn at once whether he is married. If she meets him at a public place, or through casual acquaintances, her chances of getting facts about him are limited. This is one of the main arguments for confining one's social life to acceptable circles and one's friendships to those who are vouched for upon introduction.

WHEN THE WOMAN IS OLDER

Public opinion says that the man should always be older than the girl he dates. Some girls feel this pressure of opinion so strongly that they refuse to reveal their true ages if they are indeed older than their dates. They may even deliberately falsify their ages and pretend to be younger than they are. Actually a girl can be older than the boy she dates, and a woman older than the man she marries, without any damage to the relationship unless one or the other of them makes an issue over their relative ages.

Some of the happiest marriages ever studied are those in which the woman is older than her husband. Social scientists who are concerned with interpreting interpersonal relationships feel that since marriage demands more of the woman than it does of the man (in her having to adjust to his name, his work, his place of residence, and his way of life), it helps if she's emotionally mature enough to make these adjustments in a grown-up way. Being the older of the two, she is, theoretically at least, more mature and so is able to work out a mutually satisfying relationship. Although nothing quite parallel has ever been studied among dating pairs, the situation may operate similarly. An older girl is not quite so apt to be demanding, jealous, and possessive. She may have much to give the boy in the way of social poise that will eventually help them both. She may appreciate him more than would someone his own age or younger.

The most important factor seems to be the two people's own feelings about their difference in ages. If an older woman is always afraid that she'll lose her man to some younger female, or if she "lords it over him" because she's wiser and more experienced, there may be trouble. If, on his side, he makes her feel vulnerable by teasing her about her age, or if he takes a dependent role and lets her manage things and him, the relationship may founder. But if two people can understand that the number of birthdays a person has had is far less important than the quality of the life he has lived, age differences are no longer a legitimate concern.

THE BOYS IN UNIFORM

There once was considerable stigma about dating a man in uniform. Now, when most boys experience military service before they are far into their twenties, the situation is changed. A young man joins the service and soon finds himself in a training post far removed from the friends and associates of his home town. Some impulsive young fellows take this opportunity to cut up and do things they would never dream of doing at home. But for the great majority, the man in uniform is still the same man he was at home, with the same standards, values, and attitudes he always had.

The boy in uniform may be quite as fine as any home-town boy, but he poses problems for the girl who dates him. First of all, he comes from another locale, possibly a different culture, and this social gulf can cause difficulties in a relationship. Secondly, it's difficult for a girl to know what kind of person she's dealing with, since she has had no contact with his family. Thirdly, he's usually stationed in the training post for a short period of time, and there is not time enough to build a long-lasting relationship. And lastly, being away from home and friends, the young man is quite possibly lonely and especially eager for female companionship, with the result that he's overly susceptible to emotional entanglements. In

that case, what he thinks is love may be only a temporary
need.

A girl tends to date a serviceman for several reasons. (1)
She knew the boy before he got into service and so continues
her friendship with him while he's in uniform. (2) She meets
him through mutual friends in the same way she meets civil-
ians. (3) She is concerned about the plight of servicemen in
her home town and does what she can through her USO,
church, or other group to make the boys in uniform feel welcome. (4) She doesn't rate with home-town boys and dates
servicemen as the only ones that she can get. It is this fourth
group of girls whose behavior with men in service so often
gives a black eye to all. The other types of service-dates can
be as wholesome and satisfactory as the individual persons
make them.

In general it is safer to date servicemen met at church or
other well-sponsored functions which attract self-respecting

and respectable young people. A young man in uniform usually behaves the same where he's stationed as he did back
home. If he frequented poolrooms and public dance halls at
home, that will be the kind of place to which he will gravitate

no matter where he is stationed. The studious young man will search out the library when he gets a leave. The serviceman who grew up enjoying Y youth group functions will be on the alert for announcements of similar activities. This is why you must go to the right places to meet the right people. The boy you meet in a tavern may be as fine a person as the serviceman you meet at a church social, but the chances are that more conventional behavior will be found under church auspices than under the influence of alcohol.

SUMMING UP

The difference in age or status between members of a dating couple is important only to the extent that it influences a relationship. The important thing is that a couple enjoy each other's company, share enough interests so that they can build a relationship around mutual activities, and see eye to eye on enough of life so that they are a real pair.

THE RIGHT DATE FOR YOU

Young people are rightly concerned about whom to date and whom *not* to date. Get a good date, and you have fun, your parents approve, and your friends welcome you to social affairs. Get someone your parents and friends dislike, or someone you don't find companionable, and you can have a miserable time. Sometimes it also happens that the person your parents consider a fine date leaves you cold, and the one you would like to date just doesn't rate with your friends and family. Then what?

WHEN PARENTS DISAPPROVE

Whether they know your date or not, your parents may disapprove of him or her. They may not like your date's family and background. They may believe that there is too great an age difference between the two of you. They may be concerned about differences in religion, nationality, or social and economic background. They may have heard something unfavorable about your date or his family. Or they may disapprove of *anyone* in whom you're interested, simply because they don't want to see you involved with anyone yet. Whatever the reasons for parents' disapproval, the problem is a real one.

Young people themselves generally agree that dating on the sly is not a good solution to the problem of parents' disapproval. Someone is sure to discover the situation, and parents become doubly aroused over the deception. Defying your parents and dating the person of whom they disapprove is apt to be unpleasant for everyone concerned. Yielding to parents' wishes and refraining from dating anyone of whom they disapprove can be limiting; sometimes, unfortunately, even prejudiced and restricting. Young people argue that they should have the right to choose their own friends without constant interference from their parents. At the same time youth generally acknowledges parents' right to be interested and concerned about their children's dating partners and patterns.

The best solution seems to be that of trying to get your

parents to see what you like in the other person and finding a mutually comfortable adjustment to the problem. It sometimes helps to reassure parents that you're not planning to get serious about everyone you date, and that you know as well as they that an individual may make a good date but a poor marriage partner. Parents often look too far ahead too soon and worry that your date will lead straight to an unfortunate marriage. If you can assume the kind of responsibility for your dating that assures your parents that you're not going off the deep end into some impossible match, you may find them relaxing about your casual friendships and dating partners.

Especially helpful, too, is the practice of getting your parents acquainted with your friends and dating partners very early in the relationship. If you and your date spend some time at home, you will provide an opportunity for both you and your parents to see how well the person in question fits in with your way of life and values.

Introducing Your Date to Your Family

A girl can ask a boy in whom she's interested to drop by her home for a Sunday afternoon TV show when conversation with her family can be relaxed and casual over a bowl of popcorn or a cup of cocoa. Parents who have had a chance to see a boy and talk with him will think of him as a person rather than just a boy in the abstract. It's up to the girl to arrange a meeting that will be most comfortable for her, the boy, and her parents.

It's customary for a boy to call for his date at her home. She greets him at the door and brings him in to meet her family. As she introduces her mother to her date, she says, "Mother, this is Jim. He's in my history class and helped me find that reference I was looking for last week." This gives

Mother some talking point with Jim. Similarly when a girl introduces a date to her father, she might say, "Dad, this is Jim. He's on the basketball team this year." If Dad has ever played basketball, there will be no pause in the conversation. A girl continues to acquaint her family with her date by dropping such little conversation-starters from time to time, and soon Jim and her folks get past that first embarrassment to a free and easy flow of talk. When the couple finally go off on their date, the girl's parents can feel more secure. They have met their daughter's escort and know by first-hand experience that he's "nice."

A boy may not find it quite as easy to arrange a meeting between his parents and a new girl, partly because it's not expected that he will bring his girl home until the relation-

ship is fairly far along. His parents can be helpful in arranging simple little outings such as picnics, fishing trips, or a backyard barbecue to which the girl may be invited along with other young people. Or the boy himself can invite a few friends over for an informal get-together, then casually introduce a new girl friend to his parents in a setting that doesn't commit anyone. Sometimes a young fellow who doesn't drive a car finds it easy for his parents to get acquainted with a girl when they chauffeur the pair to school, church, and community functions.

An older fellow who drives the family car can sometimes arrange to pick up his girl friend while he is driving his mother on an errand or taking his parents to some affair. A college boy can invite a girl, and perhaps another couple, to his home for a week end. Or he can have his parents as his guests on the campus for a Saturday game at which time they get to know the girl with whom he's going. These things can be done easily, once the persons involved grant their importance. The first and most important step is recognizing that parents have a right to be interested in your dates—and letting them in on the situation as soon as possible.

THE REALLY SMART GIRL

College and high school girls are frequently concerned about the wisdom of dating boys who are not their intellectual equals. Boys worry less about dating girls inferior to them in intellect, since it is generally expected that a girl won't be as intelligent as the boy she dates. Indeed this is emphasized so strongly that a superior girl may find that if she has a reputation as a "brain," boys are afraid to date her. Such a girl may pretend to be dumber than she is on a date. She plays up to a boy in the age-old game of making him feel superior. But there are girls who resent having to "put their brains on ice," so they go out only with boys who like them as they are, who admire intelligence and are not threatened by a girl's superior mental ability. A girl who dates a boy who is not her intellectual equal must decide whether she dares be herself or whether she must put on an act.

In time a really smart girl learns that she can enjoy different kinds of people in different ways. She discovers that flaunting her knowledge is not pleasant to anyone in any setting. She finds that even the least promising boy can be interesting when he's functioning in areas that he knows well. Such a girl is able to have a good time with whomever she is and wherever she is. By getting to know different types of people with varying abilities, she eventually discovers the intellectual level in which she feels comfortable. Eventually she selects a compatible partner for marriage.

FARM BOYS AND CITY GIRLS

There is some feeling among farm people that a farm boy should go out only with girls who have been brought up on a farm. The chief reason seems to be the fear that a city girl won't know how to perform all the jobs a farm woman is called on to do, and therefore would be unsuitable as a marriage partner. As is so often the case, adults tend to visualize a dating couple as falling in love and getting married, and so they evaluate the pair not as dates but as mates.

Nowadays, however, there is not as much difference between farm and city youth as once may have been the case. Boys and girls from farms and cities meet each other and share events in large consolidated schools. They have equal access to social affairs and activities via the family car, the same radio and television programs, and oftentimes the same college and vocational plans. Even if a relationship ends in marriage, the city girl is no longer at so serious a disadvantage on the farm because of modern equipment and labor-saving devices.

In general, evidence proves that if the two persons have real interests in common and enjoy each other as friends, the locale of their families' residences is not especially important unless someone makes an issue of it.

Farm Girls and City Fellows

Studies show that more farm girls migrate to the city than do farm boys. The question then is: Just how advisable is it for a farm girl to date a city boy? The chief concern here seems to be her ability to handle a date who is more sophisticated than she is. The old story of the traveling salesman and the farmer's daughter has some basis in the tendency of certain urban males to try to exploit the presumably more naïve country girl.

The skills and standards that generally hold for any kind of date safeguard today's farm girls from most unfortunate situations. The 4-H girl or the FHA member may be better prepared for boy-girl relationships than her city cousin because of the advantages she has had in building social skills through discussions and supervised experience in wholesome settings throughout her teen years.

DATING OUTSIDE YOUR FAITH

Should a Protestant date a Catholic? Is it wise for a Christian to date a Jew? Is there a real problem in going out with a person who belongs to a different church than yours? These are serious questions for most modern young people. There was a time in some communities when a boy or girl met only those of his own church in social affairs. Now members of many different churches are associated in school and community activities. Getting to know a person from a completely different religious background is easy today. The problem is in knowing whether to have dates with persons from such widely different backgrounds.

How Parents Feel

Parents of all religions generally prefer that their sons and daughters date within their own group. Social pressure generally operates in this direction. Date someone of your own faith and no questions are asked. Date a person from a different faith and you may be called upon to defend your choice, perhaps even fight for the right to that friendship.

There are those who argue that in a democracy like ours, unwillingness to date a person of another faith is wrong. Young people sometimes feel strongly about their right to date whomever they want, regardless of religion. They claim that the prejudices of adults should not be allowed to limit the friendships of young people. They pride themselves on their tolerance, and, upon occasion, even flaunt their interfaith friendships, further complicating the problem.

Adolescent young people who are attempting to emancipate themselves from their parents may deliberately date a person of a different faith as a way of proving that they are grown up and can choose their own companions. Unconsciously, they may prefer the other individual just because their parents *do* disapprove. As he grows more mature, a young person doesn't have to defy his parents quite so flagrantly, and the charm of difference for difference' sake wears off.

When two persons see a lot of each other in dating situations it's always possible that the relationship will become so emotionally or sexually involved that the couple is forced into marriage whether they are well matched as a pair or not. Thus it is understandable that parents feel easier when dates are restricted to members of their own or a similar church.

Value of Interfaith Dating

It can be argued that a well-balanced young person can learn a great deal from dating persons of different faiths. He learns to appreciate different types of people and to understand something of other religions. He broadens, too, in his awareness of the essential similarities among peoples of all religious groups. He may lose something of the early, narrowly focused belief that his church is the only true religion and develop a reverence for all men of good will from whatever church they come.

Problems in Interfaith Dating

The young dating pair from different churches may start out with the feeling that what they do is no one else's business. Then as they become fonder of each other, they feel that their love is worth any problem that may arise from the differences in their religion. Later, as they feel the full force of opposition from their friends and families, they have to decide whether they can stand the pressure which is building up against them.

If you seriously date someone outside your faith, you must *honestly* face whether you are strong enough to take all the conflict which the future will bring. Can each of you weather the chill blasts of nonacceptance in many areas of your social life? One or both of you may be excluded. Will you be able to win a real place for yourselves in the inner circle of each other's family? How will you meet problems of whose church is your church? And which church will be your children's? Such questions should be thrashed out by a couple long before the actual situations arise.

Refusing to face the problems as well as the challenges of

dating and possibly marrying outside one's religion is merely dodging the issue. Even though the questions may be complex and the solutions elusive, some decisions must be made if the relationship continues.

Couples dating outside their religious faith would do well to talk over their problems and possible decisions with an understanding counselor. He could help them see what values are worth preserving and what courses of action will work best for them. Such a counselor could be anyone in whom the two persons have confidence. It could be a minister, a priest, or a rabbi. It may be some sympathetic older relative. It could be a parent or an older sister or brother. Discussions with others of your own age are often helpful too, especially if they occur in well-led school classes, church forums, or Y programs. Reading what has been written about dating and marrying outside one's religious faith will not answer all questions for you, but it can stimulate thought and wholesome action.

Parents are justified in their concern over interfaith unions. There is evidence that many mixed marriages do not work out as happily or as permanently as marriages within the same religious group. There are successful interfaith marriages, of course, but they are generally more difficult to work out than are marriages within the same faith.

CROSSING LINES OF NATIONALITY OR RACE

Much that has been said about interfaith dating applies as well to dating members of other nationalities and racial groups. Social pressure tends to oppose it. Young people who consciously or unconsciously want to defy their parents may seek out such dates as one way of declaring their independence. The solution comes through consideration by the two persons of the merits of the particular situation, as sensibly as possible, perhaps in consultation with an understanding counselor.

There are great regional differences in the acceptance of members of a particular race or nationality as dates. In certain sections of the country feeling runs high against intermixtures that might be tolerated elsewhere. To run in the face of intense social pressure in such a community is to find oneself an outcast by members of both cultural groups.

In the years since World War II when so many of our most marriageable young men have been stationed in faraway places, it is understandable that many of them have associated with and eventually married girls of other nationalities and races. In many cases the foreign bride is taken under the wing of her mother-in-law when the couple return to this country. If the boy's mother accepts his foreign bride, the couple have a good chance of working out a stable marriage. If there is bitterness and ill-feeling over the marriage on the part of either family, the couple may be in for a rough time.

The majority of young people tend to associate within their own nationality and racial group—in dates as in marriage. These more homogeneous combinations of dating pairs and married couples do not have as wide a cultural gulf to span in their relationship. So it follows that building a harmonious relationship is easier for them than if they were associated with persons from widely different backgrounds.

GETTING INTO ANOTHER SOCIAL CLASS

Hollingshead's study of dating pairs in a Midwestern high school found that the great majority of young people dated with persons of about the same social class. When a boy dates a girl of another social class, she is usually from a class lower in the social scale than his own. Occasionally a girl dates a boy who is "beneath her." Therefore, the question of whether it's advisable to date persons from other social and economic groups is a real one for young people of both sexes and of all social groupings.

When the boy on the hill dates the girl from across the tracks, the general public is apt to assume that it's because she is willing to let him take more liberties with her than would a girl from his own social group. This may or may not be true, depending on the girl involved, but the suspicion

still remains and the couple have to battle the fears of family and friends, whether the doubts are justified or not.

Making a "Good Marriage"

Convention has it that a girl should "better herself" if possible when she dates and marries. When she marries into a family higher in the social scale than her own, she is said to "marry up" or to have "made a good marriage." In such a situation her parents are usually pleased with her choice, and sometimes even brag to their friends about how well their daughter has done. Even so, there are real problems in dating and marrying outside one's own group, as many real-life and fictional portrayals have shown.

Kitty Foyle, it will be remembered, faced the opposition of members of the old Philadelphia family to which her lover belonged. A girl from humble surroundings may not have the social graces, the clothes, or the friends that are considered important by the higher-placed boy's family. As long as she goes with boys of her own social level, lacks in conversational ability or social skills are not so important, but when she gets in with a set where such things are valued highly, she may find herself at a distinct disadvantage. Of course, if she faces these facts squarely and does something more than stew about them, she can achieve social poise in time.

As all of us become more truly democratic we realize that the amount of money a family has or the kind of car one drives is no measure of the real worth of the person. A girl from a modest family may have spiritual sensitivities and ethical values as well as cultural interests that can greatly enrich the life of the wealthy fellow she is dating or planning to marry. It may also be that a poor boy with real talent can be given just the boost he needs to realize his full potential, by the financial aid of a girl who loves him.

Many a girl has become interested in an ambitious boy not in her social group, and has gone with him because she has faith in him. She often tries to help him get ahead, by urging her father to give him a chance in his business or by encouraging him to go on with his education. Such a relationship can be rewarding to both members of the pair, but it has its hazards too.

Problems That Arise

One problem that arises is that the girl's other friends do not fully accept "the outsider" and tend to freeze out both him and the girl who has befriended him. Still another problem arises when the boy finds it hard on his ego to take all the help that his girl wants to give him. The girl's family may oppose her dating a boy who is beneath her social level. Even the boy's family may object to his associating with people who don't accept him or them.

For these reasons most dates tend to be between persons of about the same social level. It is possible to date, and eventually to marry, an individual from another social and economic level; indeed it is done every day. But such relationships are less frequent and can be more difficult to maintain harmoniously than are those within the same general social group.

YOUR FRIENDS' OPINIONS

A high school girl asks, "If your friends do not approve of a boy, can you afford to go with him?" She goes on to tell of how only she, of her whole group of pals, is interested in Joe. She wonders whether she should go with Joe in the face of her friends' disapproval or whether she should follow their advice and give him up.

The answer to such a question depends upon several factors. First of all, why don't her friends approve of the boy? What is it about Joe that Marion likes? How much do Marion's friends mean to her? How much does the boy mean? Could she stand losing her friends if need be over Joe? Or are they so important to her that she couldn't give them up?

This is not an uncommon problem among both fellows and

girls. Often it is tied up with the larger question of dating someone with a bad reputation and can be understood more clearly in that context.

THAT BAD REPUTATION

It is the social group that determines what is a bad reputation. In one social set a girl can get a bad reputation for smoking and drinking. In another crowd a different set of behaviors is "bad." A boy who dates such a girl with a bad reputation, and vice versa, is running the risk of having some of her reputation rub off on him.

One problem about dating a person with a bad reputation is that you may not be sure whether the charge is justified. The grapevine says that a certain girl is *persona non grata,* and yet from what you see of her, she seems nice. Conversely, a boy may have a bad reputation among your friends and yet from your own contact with him, he seems courteous and gentlemanly. How are you to know?

There are several factors to consider before you let someone's reputation influence you to turn down a date. In the first place, you must realize that a person may have been unjustly accused of something he did not do. Secondly, the person's unfavorable reputation may be based on prejudice against his family, his race, or his social standing, rather than upon his own character. Thirdly, it's only fair that every individual be given another chance, and if no one befriends him, he never gets that chance to make something of himself. Lastly, it's possible for a girl to raise the standards of her date or improve his reputation, and in that way help a boy to reclaim himself. To behave with such objectivity and compassion is worthy, but a person must still face the problems encountered in dating someone whose reputation is not good.

The biggest problem in dating someone whom others shun is that you too may be avoided because of your association with that individual. Then, instead of helping the other person, you are only hurting yourself.

Another problem not quite so easily recognized is that your motivation for associating with a person with a bad reputation may be based upon your conscious or unconscious wish to hurt or offend your friends or family. A girl may date a boy of whom she knows her family disapproves, just to spite them. She acts out of a need to defy her parents and to rebel from their control, and not because of sympathy for the boy. A fellow may date a girl of whom his friends disapprove, not so much because he likes her, but to show his friends that he can date whomever he wants without their interference. This kind of behavior is childish and unfortunate, both for the individual who is flaunting his independence and for the one who is being dated. It rarely helps the one with the bad reputation, and it is often ruinous for the one acting out of defiance and rebellion.

HOW CAN YOU JUDGE?

The big question for many young people is: How can you judge another person? Should a girl judge a boy by what her family says about him or by what she knows of him? Should a boy judge a girl by what people say about her or by what he sees in her? Or both? How much should one listen to others in judging an individual? And how much can one trust one's own judgment in appraising another's personality? These are difficult questions to answer, especially when we realize how much is at stake in the reputation and the future happiness of the persons involved.

There is no denying that each of us as individuals has

both a character and a reputation. Your character is what you really are. Your reputation is what others think and say about you. Sometimes your reputation coincides with your character—then there's no problem. Oftentimes your reputation is not a true reflection of your character, and injustice is done.

In a religious country, we believe that any individual who makes a mistake should be allowed to repent, to make amends for whatever damage he has done insofar as he can, and then be given the right to reclaim himself. We recognize that no one of us is perfect, and that from time to time each of us needs a chance to make things right again.

If we take such religious teachings seriously we cannot blindly follow the prejudices that build up against certain individuals and groups. But seeing a person sincerely trying to improve makes us want to give him our encouragement and friendship.

This does not mean that social opinions and pressures are not important—they are. You cannot shrug off a person's reputation as unimportant, for it is a part of him or her. The principle at stake is the right of an individual to make moral choices for himself, without blindly following the herd.

The best single answer, then, to the question of how one can judge another person as a potential dating partner is: Listen to what others say of him but also see for yourself what kind of individual he really seems to be. If on the basis of your own most mature judgment this seems to be a person worthy of your friendship, then perhaps you have the problem of "selling" him to your family and friends. They will be impressed if they feel you listen to their side too before arriving at an opinion. By giving the person you are championing a chance to prove himself in the eyes of people who are important to you, you may further your cause.

At times you may make mistakes in judging others. You may befriend someone only to get terribly hurt in the process. This is a risk we all take as human beings. In the long run it's probably better to think well of others, even at the risk of getting hurt by them once in a while, than to distrust other people unjustly and live a life of suspicion, isolation, and prejudice.

QUALITIES PREFERRED

When students at the University of Michigan listed the qualities they preferred in both casual and serious dates, three items were mentioned more frequently than others by both sexes:

Emotional maturity
Dependability
Well-roundedness

All of the men said that when they dated seriously they preferred a girl who "has good sense and is an intelligent conversationalist." College men also seek girls who are "honest and straightforward, willing to join a group, and have polished manners."

Both men and women students tend to prefer dating partners who "are good listeners, get along with friends of their own sex, and are ambitious and energetic."

These characteristics of a good date preferred by university students are not markedly different from those that high school students mention most frequently in surveys of their dating preferences. One recent nationwide sample of high

school students found that they wanted a date to be someone who

—is physically and mentally fit
—is dependable and can be trusted
—takes pride in personal appearance and manners
—is clean in speech and action
—has a pleasant disposition and sense of humor
—is considerate of others
—acts own age and not childish

QUALITIES DISLIKED

Boys tend to be criticized more often than girls for being vulgar in speech and action, for wanting too much necking and petting, for withholding compliments, for being careless in dress and manners, and for being disrespectful of the other sex.

Girls in the same nationwide survey of some 8,000 teenagers are criticized for being easily hurt, shy and self-conscious, emotionally cold, too possessive, and for acting childish and silly. In general, both sexes agree that these criticisms are justified and are problems in dating.

SUMMING UP

A good date for you is someone in whom you have faith, someone whose company you enjoy and who enjoys your companionship in return, someone you are proud to be seen with. If your family and friends approve of your choice, that is fine. If they don't, you may be headed for trouble with them, with your date, or with both. What you do when you come up against such problems depends in large measure on the kind of person you are, and what your real reasons are for choosing a particular dating partner.

5

ASKING FOR A DATE

Some people find it easy to ask for a date. But for many young people this is a very complicated process. How far in advance should you ask? What shall you say? What if she says "No"? These and many other questions are asked by young men all over the country. Even some fellows who have been dating for quite a while are still unsure of the proper approach in asking for dates. Girls as well as boys are faced with this problem as they take the initiative. There are no clear-cut answers to these questions, but here are some factors to consider when planning to ask for a date.

ADVANCE NOTICE

The amount of advance notice recognized as appropriate in asking for a date depends upon the specific event planned. If you're asking a girl to a party at school or church, or club, you'll want to give her more notice than if you're just taking her to a movie or a ball game. Try to plan your invitation far enough in advance to give the girl opportunity to prepare for the event. If you're inviting her to a formal dance, she will need time to plan and buy her outfit. Boys, too, need time to prepare themselves for a special event. In general, it

71

is wise to give notice of two weeks or more for a big affair. For a main prom, you might ask two or three months in advance.

Especially if you'd like to date a certain girl, it's to your advantage to ask her some time in advance. If she's a girl who has many dates, the earlier you ask, the more chance you have of finding her free that evening. It sometimes takes a while to get up the courage to ask a girl to a special function. But proper planning will make it a lot easier for both of you. And it will be a wonderful feeling to have your date all lined up when other boys are still wondering whom to ask, and "Will she go with me?" Your date appreciates too the security of an early invitation.

Movie dates, or dates to functions where extensive preparation is not necessary, don't require as much advance notice. At the same time, it's good to extend your invitation a week or so ahead of time if you want to be sure of getting your date. A girl appreciates this kindness, for it enables her to schedule her week end to include your date, without having to exclude other activities which may also be important to her.

Spur-of-the-Moment Dates

This doesn't mean that spur-of-the-moment dates are not acceptable. If you and your friends get together and suddenly decide to go skating or to a show, it's perfectly all right to call and ask a girl to accompany you. The girl who feels insulted or rejects such an invitation just because it's at the last moment may find herself left out in the cold eventually, missing a lot of fun. Many a girl enjoys the spontaneity of dropping what she is doing and getting into the swing of a skating party or wienie roast.

Second-Choice Dates

Sometimes you have a date for an affair and something unforeseen happens so that your date cannot make it at the last minute. Then you are in the awkward position of calling another girl—especially awkward if she knows you already had a date. If a girl stops to realize, however, how many "second choices" you had to select from, she will not be hurt. She will be pleased, instead, that you chose her and will accept your invitation. In such a case it helps greatly to let a girl know that you really like her as a person and are not inviting her just because you couldn't get someone else. Many "second choices," who have been mature enough not to resent being "second choice," have ended up as "first choices" later.

ALTERNATIVES IN ASKING

There are two usual ways of asking for a date. You can phone a girl at her home or you can ask her in person. Each way has its own advantages, and the method you use depends upon your own taste and whom you are asking out. Sometimes you may have to write to ask for a date. If, for instance, you want a girl to come and visit you at college, you will most likely send her an invitation by mail. In most instances, however, invitations are issued either in person or by phone. Which of these two methods is more satisfactory depends upon you and your surroundings.

In Person

Sometimes you can have more privacy if you ask the girl in person. If you have a teasing brother at home, or if your girl has a little sister who likes to listen in on the extension phone, you may prefer seeing her alone when you ask for a date. Certainly this would be true if your phone is on a party line, where neighbors might listen in on your conversation.

When you're walking her home after class is a good time to ask. Or perhaps over a Coke after school. It's not fair to yourself or to your prospective date to ask her while other people are standing around listening. This is a private matter between you and her.

By Phone

People who feel self-conscious with the other sex often find it easier to ask for a date by phone. Some fellows get tongue-tied when they talk with girls, and it's not nearly as pronounced or noticeable over the phone. Also asking via telephone gives a boy time to plan his invitation. He can even write out just what he's going to say, so that if he does falter he'll have his memo to fall back on.

From the girl's point of view, if she's called at her home, she has more opportunity to ask for her parents' consent without giving a boy the impression that she's stalling. She'll also have pad and pencil at hand to jot down the details of the date and avoid misunderstandings later.

In asking for a date, some people prefer to begin by discussing something unrelated until they feel more at ease. If you're calling someone who is in one of your classes, you might start off with a remark about something that occurred in class that day. It's not wise, however, to drag this preliminary chitchat on too long. A girl may be in the midst of her homework and not have time to talk at length. Or her parents may object to long phone tie-ups. As soon as you've established a little confidence, get to the invitation.

Be Specific

One of the most important things to remember in asking for a date is to be specific. State in full just what your invitation is, where you are going, what day and hour it is, when it will be over, whether you are going with others, and if so, with whom. It's not fair to call and ask a girl what she's doing Saturday night; she wants to know what you're planning on doing Saturday night!

Expect an Answer

As soon as you've told her all about the date, expect an answer. In most cases she will be able to tell you right then and there whether or not she can accept. If she's not sure (perhaps she must ask her parents first), then you can make a definite deadline for her reply. There's no reason for her to stall. Out of fairness to a boy, a girl should either accept or refuse—or else explain why she cannot answer immediately and state a time when he may expect her reply.

Be Courteous

As you ask a girl for a date, you should indicate that you really want to go with her. Courtesy is very important when asking, for if the girl finds you are not too courteous on the phone, she may assume you're also discourteous on dates. A typical phone call for a date might be something like this:

MARY: Hello.

JIM: Hi, Mary, this is Jim Jones.

MARY: Hi, Jim, how are you?

JIM: Fine, thanks. Say, did you understand that problem in math today? I found it rather confusing.

MARY: I did too, but I eventually figured it out.

JIM: So did I. Say, Mary, Bob and Larry are taking Jean and Jane to the White Kar roller skating rink this Saturday—about seven o'clock. I'd like very much to take you, and we'd be home by ten. Would you like to go?

MARY: It sounds like fun! I'd love to go skating with you, Jim. I'll expect you Saturday about seven.

JIM: Fine, see you then. Good-by, Mary.

MARY: Good-by.

This conversation was a great help to Mary. She knows everything she needs to know. Mary knows that Jim really wants to take her skating. She knows that she should dress casually, and that she should be ready by seven. She can tell her parents that she will be home by ten. This is the kind of invitation she likes to receive, because nothing is left up in the air. He told her who he was at once, instead of playing childish "Guess-who-this-is" games. No girl likes to admit that she doesn't recognize a boy's voice, yet many voices sound similar over the phone.

Mary's parents like this approach too. They know just what they can expect without having to quiz Jim when he comes to pick her up for the date. They like to know where their daughter is going and with whom, but they hate to give a boy the third degree before a date—just as much as a boy hates to get it.

Jim also feels happy about this conversation. He knows that Mary will be dressed for skating, and that her parents understand about the arrangements. He can also tell his parents when to expect him home. Dates with arrangements agreed on ahead of time are more fun. You can look forward to your plans, rather than wonder what you're going to do and whether you'll be dressed appropriately.

Make Plans

If you have no definite plan in mind when you ask for a date, you both can discuss what you would like to do. Offer several different suggestions (within your budget) for her to choose from. But don't ask a girl to tell you what she wants to do without giving her some idea of the amount of money you have to spend. You'll be putting her on the spot—and possibly yourself too. You don't want to embarrass either yourself or your date by having her select a place that is beyond your financial means. Being honest about the amount of money you can spend avoids misunderstandings later.

In general, it's better not to wait until you get to a girl's house to decide what you're going to do. Advance planning will avoid the embarrassment of inappropriate clothing or budget problems.

If She Says "No"

Sometimes, even if a girl would like to go out with you, she must refuse your invitation. But usually you can tell by her attitude whether it's just this date she cannot accept, or whether you would be wasting your time calling her again. If she says she's terribly sorry—she would like to go to the game with you but she has promised to baby-sit that night—you probably ought to ask her again sometime. If she implies that she'd rather not date you, calling again might be useless and only make you unhappy.

It's no fun to be turned down for a date. It helps if you know the real reason a girl refuses. If she says that she has a previous commitment, you can accept that at face value and ask her for another night. If she replies that she's going to be busy for the next three weeks or so, it might mean that you had better start looking elsewhere for a more available date.

If a girl refuses a date without giving a reason, don't press for an answer. It can be embarrassing if a girl has a personal reason for refusing and the boy pesters for an explanation. Perhaps she's not been well and doesn't want to do anything strenuous. Maybe she is menstruating and can't go swimming. It may be that she doesn't know how to skate, and rather than tell you, she refuses the date. If she says she can't see you that particular night, but in her attitude tells you that she likes you as a person, you might ask her to some different type of activity the next time or offer alternative suggestions. This way you'll learn something of her interest and availability.

GETTING HIM TO ASK YOU FOR A DATE

Many young women get discouraged when they see datable young men who never seem to go out. Other young men date, but just fail to notice many very nice girls who'd like to go out with them. Girls all over the country often ask, "How do you get a boy to ask you for a date?"

When interested in a special boy who has not asked you out, the first thing to try to discover is why. There are many different reasons why boys do not date, or do not date specific girls, and if you know what they are it will be helpful. Sometimes it's not easy to determine a boy's reason for not dating you, but often you can tell from his attitude, or from listening to others, what is behind his indifference.

Maybe He's Shy

Many girls are faced with the problem of a boy who is too shy or unsure of himself to ask them for a date. Letting him know that you like him in a discreet, unshowy way may help draw him out of his shell. Without chasing him, you can be friendly and courteous and let him know that you think he is datable. You might take the initiative the first time or so and invite him to a party at your house, or ask him over some Sunday afternoon to help make candy. Find out what his interests are and be a good listener. Most boys relax when they start to talk about things with which they are familiar. As soon as they realize that you're interested in some of the same things they are, they'll seek you out for company.

Maybe He Hasn't Noticed You

What can you do about a fellow who dates girls but just doesn't notice you? Well, acting in a loud conspicuous manner will make him notice you, but it will work in the wrong direction as far as making you datable in his eyes. What you have to do is be friendly without being a "clinging vine." You have to look appealing without being considered "flashy." You can be feminine and yet be versatile enough to fit into a hike, a skating or biking party.

The next time you're at a party with this boy who doesn't notice you, make it a point to be friendly. Don't just hang back in a corner wishing he would ask you for a dance. Talk with him. Let him know you're there without forcing yourself on him. Get him to talk about himself. Many girls who could never get to first base with a boy suddenly made a hit when he discovered they would listen to his enthusiastic talk about baseball or motorboats. If he still doesn't ask you to go out with him, you can be sure it's not because he hasn't noticed you but because there's some other reason.

Maybe He Has Other Interests

Some boys become so involved with outside interests that they just can't spare any time for girls. For instance, maybe Bob has an old car he's fixing up. Such a hobby is very time-consuming, and he may consider it more important at this time than dating. Maybe he works after school and comes home too tired to go out. What do you do then? Well, you might try showing an interest in what he likes to do. If he must go home every afternoon to work on his car, maybe you'd like to don a pair of jeans and offer to be an apprentice. He'll probably appreciate your help and interest, and he may suddenly realize that you're quite a gal! Of course, even this might not bring him around to the place where he thinks he can spare time for dates. In that case, you invite him to a party—at your house some afternoon. If even this doesn't work, you may just have to accept his not being ready to date yet. But it was fun trying, wasn't it? And besides, you may have learned something interesting about cars!

The boy who works after school is an entirely different problem. It's perfectly understandable that a young man who attends classes and then has to work may very well be too

tired to do much of anything in the evening. However, you might try to arrange to do your homework together. Or perhaps he would go to a picnic with you some Sunday afternoon. If he hasn't dated much, don't expect him to jump into the swing of dating on week nights—he just can't. But if you're nice to him now, he may remember you on his occasional free week ends and surprise you by calling for a date.

Maybe He Has Another Girl

There's no use pining over a boy who's going steady with another girl. For the time being they probably have eyes only for each other. And it's no help to get a reputation as a "man-snatcher." No one has respect for them. This doesn't mean that you can't be nice to such a fellow, but don't keep after him for a date, because you'll probably just get hurt in the long run. Should he break up with his girl later on, you can help him get back into circulation by being friendly. But don't be pushy—he may still be bitter about his previous experience.

Maybe He's Too Popular

Some boys just naturally seem to be popular, even too popular. There's no point in aiming for the most popular boy in the class if you haven't dated much before. You'll only cause yourself heartaches. At the same time, don't avoid a boy just because he dates a lot of other girls. One of these days he may realize that you're a pretty cute girl and that he'd like to see more of you. If you prove your eligibility by dating other boys, he's more likely to notice you in the future.

GIRL ASKS BOY

More and more occasions come up where a girl has to ask a boy for a date. Many girls' clubs have dances and parties which are girl-ask-boy affairs. And girls are usually the party-givers—boys the party-goers, after they've been asked! The technique of asking a boy for a date is quite similar to the procedure when a boy asks a girl. Mary gives Jim specific information as to what the invitation is, where the affair is to be held, who will be there, the day and hour it will take place, and whether she expects him to call for her at her home.

In addition, it's good practice to tell a boy just what will be expected of him when he takes you to this affair. If he's driving and you want him to take another couple with you, it will help him plan his time if he knows this fact beforehand. He'll also want to tell his parents where he'll be and approximately when he'll be home. If there's anything in the invitation that might cost him money, let him know this too, so that you both will avoid embarrassment later.

SUMMING UP

When asking for a date, both boys and girls do best if they extend their invitations well in advance. They are specific in their invitations. They act natural. And they indicate that the person they're asking out is the one they really want to take. Dating becomes even more fun when it's anticipated with the warm feeling that comes from a sincere invitation.

ACCEPTING OR REFUSING
A DATE

Whether to accept or refuse a date is not as clear-cut as it might seem at first glance. Many young women have questions regarding whether they should accept a specific invitation and how they should refuse if it is necessary. Girls are especially eager to find some way of refusing a date without hurting the

84

feelings of the boy involved. Even if she doesn't care to date him at all, it's still a good idea for her to decline the invitation in such a way that the boy will not feel hurt. If you're rude or inconsiderate of a young man's feelings, the word gets about. Other young men whom you might like to date may hesitate to call you because of a fear that you'll be rude to them too.

If you would like to accept a date but have a previous commitment, you will want to find some way of letting the boy know that you would really like to go out with him. If you just say you're sorry that you can't make it, the boy may decide you don't want to date him at all. So you refuse this invitation and yet let the boy know that you would be interested some other time.

Even accepting a date can be complicated. How can you let Steve know that you're very happy to go out with him without seeming overeager? How can you show him that you're sincerely interested in going with him, and not just using him as a free ticket to an event? Your attitude when accepting or refusing a date can greatly influence boys in giving future invitations.

One of the first problems that girls face when receiving an invitation is whether or not they should (or can) accept. If you have a previous engagement for that night, there's no question—you must refuse. If you have that night free, here are some factors to consider before accepting a date.

STOP TO INVESTIGATE

If a boy you have never dated before invites you out, you may have many questions which you'd like answered before giving him your reply. Even if you know the boy well, it's a good idea to get a thorough understanding of what the date entails before accepting his invitation. Before accepting any date, here are some things you would do well to consider.

First of all, what do you know about the boy? Have you been out with him before? Did he prove to be trustworthy in getting you home when promised? It's not fun to be on a date and spend the evening worrying about your escort. If you're not sure that this particular young man can be trusted, the date won't be a very happy one.

Girls just starting to date will want to be particularly careful. If the boys they go out with are much older or much more experienced, situations may arise that they're not prepared to handle. Awkward moments develop if a boy expects more of his date than she is able and willing to give. The girl may actually be in physical danger if the boy does not respect her values.

If you do not personally know the boy who's requesting a date, what *do* you know about him? Have you heard good things about him through the grapevine? Do you know someone who is familiar enough with him to give you an opinion?

If he's not the type of person you would feel comfortable dating, your answer to his invitation is clear. If you like him as a person, or would like to know him better, you may want to consider some other things before deciding.

"I Know Where I'm Going"

The place you're invited to makes a difference. If the invitation is for a function at school, church, community center, or Y, you can feel comfortable in accepting the invitation. A movie or a sports event can also be lots of fun. If, however, the invitation is to a place that you know nothing or little about, you might feel better if you found out about it before giving your answer. Public dance halls, places where alcohol is served, and parties at homes where you do not know the hostess can be hazardous. Find out as much as you can about the place you are invited to before you accept. If you can't find out by yourself, ask your parents or your house mother. They will probably know whether or not it is the type of place for you.

Check and Double Check

If you are asked out on a double date, it will help if you know something about the other couple. Are they the kind of people you will have fun with? Are they also interested in avoiding embarrassing situations? If you have heard unpleasant things about this other couple, you might want to avoid the date. Likewise, if you have been asked to a party at the house of someone you don't know, you may want to check on a few things before accepting. What kind of party is it likely to be? Will there be adults present? Regardless of how carefully a party is planned, things can get out of hand if there is no adult around to help out.

A Matter for Discussion

You may be very eager to accept a date. You may like the boy very much, and the place and people promise to be fun. Yet it's sometimes necessary to turn down an invitation, despite the fact that you would love to accept. If your parents disapprove, you'll have to decline the invitation regardless of other favorable factors. In such a case you might discuss the matter with your parents to find out just how they feel. If they think you are too young for regular dates, they might be willing to have you attend parties and school functions. Try to find out ahead of time just what their attitude is so that you will not be embarrassed or disappointed later.

A PROMISE IS A PROMISE

Even as a young adult, there will be occasions when you'll have to refuse invitations. If you're not feeling well, you'll have to give a "some other time" answer. If you have already made a previous engagement, you will have to decline this one, enticing as it may be. If you have promised to baby-sit, and an invitation to something you would much rather do comes along, it's hard to refuse, but you have no alternative. If Bill invites you to a school dance, but you have already promised to go with Fred whom you don't like as well, it's a great temptation to break the prior date. In the long run, however, you will find it pays off to keep your promises, even if it means missing out occasionally on something you would like to do.

WITH GOOD REASON

If you feel that you must turn down an invitation, you are faced with the problem of how to refuse without hurting the boy's feelings. Here are some tips that may help:

When there is a specific reason why you cannot accept an invitation, it's a good idea to explain if possible. A boy will appreciate your being frank and honest about how you feel. If you have a previous engagement for that evening, it is better to say so than to give a simple "No" answer.

You may have a very good reason for refusing, but unless you tell the boy what it is, he is liable to get the idea that you would rather not date him at all. It may be that you want to go out with the boy some other time; then it's especially important to give him the right impression. If you can't go out —for a personal reason you would rather not explain—try to refuse in a manner which will not hurt the boy's feelings. If you don't care what this boy feels toward you, you may still find that his reaction will influence the other boys. If you are gracious and courteous in refusing, he'll communicate that to other boys.

Sometimes you may feel embarrassed about giving the reason. If you feel uncomfortable telling a boy that you're just not up to horseback riding, tell him that you can't join him today but you'd love to some other time. The boy should catch on from what you do say and be satisfied. Sometimes, however, boys are persistent in demanding an explanation. This discourtesy need not confuse you if you are prepared for it. If he demands an explanation, just say politely that you're sorry you simply cannot go this time, but maybe next week. Then begin to talk about something else that might interest him. Or better still, suggest some other type of activity in which you could participate. If he rises to the bait, you'll have a date!

Occasionally, there is no reason for refusing an invitation except that a boy is not the type you like to date. What do you say then?

Just Not Interested

In every girl's life there's at least one boy whom she would just rather not date. He may be unpleasant company, not the right age for her, a "wolf," or he may go with a gang of particularly rough fellows. Her parents may object to him because of his age, religion, or reputation. If the boy asking for a date is not the type of person you would like to go out with, it's not fair to encourage him in any way. Letting a boy know that you do not want to go out with him without being rude is a difficult thing to do. In some cases he won't take "No" for an answer, but in most instances a few courteous but firm refusals will help the boy understand that it's just "no go."

A boy should get the hint after being turned down a few times without a good reason. If he is still persistent, you may be even cooler the next time he calls, and more definite in your refusals. Perhaps instead of giving a reason you will just have to say you would rather not go. He may even get unpleasant about it, but if you remember to keep your temper and try not to hurt him, you won't feel too badly about it. The more persistent he is, the firmer you will have to be, but eventually he will catch on and look elsewhere.

In All Sincerity

Some boys discourage easily; if turned down for a date, they may not call back for fear of being disappointed again.

There are several ways to help a boy realize that it's not him you are refusing, but that you just can't make it that particular night. First of all, your voice and attitude should be warm and friendly. Secondly, you should explain just why you're unable to accept this particular invitation. If you tell him that you would just *love* to go but you're tied up that night, he will feel better about it. And if you say that you would certainly like a rain check, in all probability he will call again —and again.

Sometimes you can suggest a counterproposal to let the boy see that you are interested in him. Maybe you have to refuse this date, but in the same conversation you could invite him over sometime to listen to records. That way he will know that you're not refusing because you don't like him.

Suggesting something different for the same night can sometimes be done tactfully. If you are invited to a dance and do not dance, it might not be fair to suggest that he take you somewhere else, because he might feel trapped and resent it. But if he invites you to do something you cannot do, explain that you would love to see him but you just don't know how to manage it. Suppose he called to invite you to the stock car races and your parents don't allow you to go. If he's suggesting a single date you could explain that you are not allowed to attend the races and mention alternatives. If his plans include others, however, it's not fair to suggest something else. Of course, if he's the one to suggest another activity, then go ahead—have fun.

THE FAIR THING TO DO

Sometimes when you are asked to go out, one or more questions must be settled before you can give your answer.

Maybe you have to ask your parents first. Maybe you don't know the hostess who is giving the party and you would like time to check up before giving the boy your answer. You might want to learn more about the place you have been invited to—or about the boy who is inviting you. You may have an exam coming up which requires last-minute preparation.

In any of these cases, or others, it's perfectly justifiable to explain that you would like to go but have to postpone your final decision. If you do have to ask a boy to wait before giving him your answer, be sure to explain why. No boy will condemn you for wanting to check with your parents before agreeing to go somewhere you're not sure about. He may tease you about it if he feels insecure, but inwardly he will respect you for being the kind of person who is trying to abide by her parents' wishes.

It's not fair to keep one boy on the string while you wait to see if another boy will ask you out for Saturday night. If there is to be an event at your school to which you would like to go, you should give a definite answer to the first boy who asks you. No one appreciates a girl who keeps a date dangling while she looks for greener pastures. It's certainly not fair to the boy, for it may be too late for him to get another date by the time you decide. It's not fair to yourself, either, for once it gets around that you do this kind of inconsiderate thing, boys will look elsewhere for dates.

If you have to give a "maybe" reply, try to offer the boy an acceptable reason along with it, and a definite time by which he may expect your answer. He will be much more able to accept your indefinite answer if he knows just when he will receive your final reply. By telling him the reason for the delay, and giving him an indication of when you will have your answer (naturally it will be as soon as possible), he will realize that you are not just "stalling."

LOOKING FORWARD TO IT

Accepting an invitation is not just a matter of saying "Yes." You want to communicate to the boy asking you just how much you would really like to go with him. Your attitude in accepting his invitation can set the tone for the coming date. Here is something you will want to remember:

Accept graciously. Let the boy know how happy you will be to go out with him. If you respond to his request with a hesitant "I guess I can go," he may feel uneasy and apprehensive about the coming date. He may even wish he had not asked you. If, however, you let the boy know that you would really enjoy going with him, he will feel more secure and look forward to the date with eager anticipation. The girl who accepts an invitation saying, "I am so glad you asked me" or "I am looking forward to it," is one the boys will be eager to ask again.

Getting Things Clear

When you're accepting a date, it's good procedure to repeat your understanding of the arrangements. If you're sure that you are completely clear on what the date entails, you will avoid misunderstandings when the time comes. If the particulars of the date are involved, you may wish to jot down some notes about it so that you won't forget. Some girls keep a little date book to avoid any chance of mix-ups. Girls in college sometimes jot down the dates of their exams so that when they are asked for a date, they can tell at a glance how full their schedule will be.

It's no fun to be ready way ahead of the time of your date's arrival. You will start your date more relaxed, however, if you allow plenty of time to dress. Your date doesn't like to be kept waiting while you finish primping. For this reason, you should know just when he will pick you up and plan to be ready at that time. If you both have a clear understanding on this point, the strain of anxious waiting will be lessened.

BROKEN DATE

Most young women today have learned that it's not good practice to break a date without good reason. Breaking a date just because you don't feel like going, or because you've had a better offer, is not only discourteous; it can do real harm. Any boy will feel hurt at such rude behavior. If he is a shy boy, he will be even more insecure in the future. Few things are more deflating to the ego than to have someone break a date without a reason. Breaking dates can be harmful to the girl also. As word gets around that she is a date-breaker, fewer and fewer boys will risk asking her out. No one wants to be left stranded at the last minute.

Regardless of how hard we try, sometimes a date must be broken at the last minute. You might have suddenly become ill. Maybe your parents have come to visit you at the dorm unexpectedly. Maybe you have a suddenly announced test in the morning for which you are not prepared. Whatever the reason for breaking a date, you will want to be honest about it when you tell the boy. It's not a good idea to feign illness as an excuse for breaking a date. This is especially true if you are planning to go out with someone else that night. If a boy can't depend upon you to tell the truth, he will soon lose interest.

If you find you do have to break a date, let the boy know as soon as you can. This will give him an opportunity to get another date. Tell him honestly why you must break the date, and if it seems appropriate, make an alternative suggestion. If he asked you to go to the movies and you're nursing an earache and can't go out in the cold, maybe you would like to invite him over to keep you company. Any boy will be flattered by this courtesy, even if he decides he would rather not come. If your date was for a dance, and you suddenly hurt your ankle, you might even offer to help him find another date. He will respect you for your effort, even if he doesn't accept it.

SUMMING UP

The same general principles apply whether you are refusing, accepting, or breaking a date. The most important thing is to be sincere and courteous. Mean what you say, and say it graciously. Be sure that a complete understanding is reached about details of the invitation. If you must refuse, try to give the reason for your refusal. If you accept, be sure that a boy understands that you really enjoy going with him. Get all the details of the date straightened out ahead of time to avoid the embarrassment of a misunderstanding. With practice, your approach for handling date offers will become more and more gracious. As you feel more at ease and secure in your abilities to handle such situations, you will naturally make the boys more eager to ask you for dates.

7

DATING—HOW OFTEN?
HOW LATE?

As soon as you begin to go out, you will face the big question of how often and how late you should date. Such questions as the following are asked by high school and college boys and girls in both large and small communities everywhere.

How many nights a week should a teen-ager go out on dates?

Should a teen-ager date on school nights?

What should a girl do if a boy wants to go out every night?
How can a girl and her family agree on an hour for her to
    get in at night?
How late is too late for a date?
What about all-night proms?

The answers to these questions depend upon the circumstances, and the people involved. Here is what teen-agers and
adults usually have to say about them.

SCHOOL-NIGHT DATING

Parents and teachers point out that when young people
date on school nights, they find it hard to get up in the morning and get off to school. Also they do not get enough sleep to
maintain good health, and they neglect their homework. Adults
generally feel that young people should restrict their dating to
week ends when they can catch up on sleep Saturday and
Sunday mornings.

When young people themselves discuss the question of how
often they may date, they tend to agree that dating is best on
week ends. Responsible fellows and girls feel that their homework comes first, and that everything works out better if they
limit their evening dating to Fridays and Saturdays. They
point out one important exception though. If there is a special
event on during the week that both the boy and the girl would
attend anyway, they might just as well enjoy it together. A
special school night, a regular band practice, or a play re-
hearsal which John and Joan must both attend becomes something of a date when it's done together. Even so, there's a
general feeling that such weekday affairs should not be late,
and that some provision should be made by young people to
get their homework done before they start out.

Sometimes you see a couple who are constantly together.

They seem to date every night in the week and spend as much of their time together as they can. Such practices are a concern to many parents and teachers, who point out the dangers of so much close association and the likelihood that one or both members of the couple are neglecting studies or other interests.

Every-Night Dating

A girl dating a boy who wants to go out more frequently than she feels is wise is in a difficult spot. She's afraid to turn him down lest he find some other girl to date. And if she's fond of the boy, she doesn't want to lose him. She may find it especially hard to curtail his dating demands because she, too, enjoys their being together.

One solution for a girl is to invite her boy friend to spend all or part of an occasional evening at home with her. She may suggest that he bring his books over so that they can do homework together. They may try to finish their assignments in time to watch some favorite television show, dance to records, or have light refreshments.

The success of such an alternative depends a great deal upon how responsible and sensible the two persons are when they are together. Some couples can get as much or more studying done together as they can do alone. Others clown around and gab so much that neither of them gets anything done.

Watch Your Welcome

On the other hand, if a boy hangs around a girl's house all the time, he may be getting her in bad with her family and neighbors. Neighbors are prone to be critical of a teen-age girl who entertains a boy too often. And even the most patient family may tire of a boy who is always underfoot. A fellow who comes to a girl's house two or even three times a week may find a warm welcome, but if he shows up every evening, that welcome may wear thin. For both his sake and the girl's, he's wise to limit the number of calls he makes to her home.

In general, it's recognized that an engaged couple, or a couple going steady, will see a great deal of each other. But even these couples find that their relationship is more acceptable to parents and friends if it's not a day-in-day-out affair that cuts out all other interests and people.

FREQUENCY OF DATING

Lowrie's study of the frequency of dating among high school and college students found several factors determining how often a given person dates. First is the factor of age. In general, between the ages of sixteen and twenty-one, the older the person, the more frequently he or she dates. Young beginning daters go out less often than those who are well established in dating patterns.

A second closely related factor is whether a teen-ager is

going steady or playing the field. As might be expected, those who go steady date much more often than those who are in circulation. College men who go steady date about twice as much as fellows who go out with many different girls. Among college girls, those who are engaged or are going steady date much more frequently than those playing the field.

A third factor is that of the age at which the young person began to date. In general, the earlier university students began their dating, the more frequently they dated in college.

Other factors affecting frequency of dating are: (1) absorption in vocational and avocational interests; (2) responsibilities for educational progress (such as is felt by the student in exacting professional training); (3) pressure of family obligations (such as care of younger sisters and brothers); (4) degree of acceptance among other young people (the popular person goes on more dates than the boy or girl who hasn't won the full acceptance of his peers); and (5) how much the particular individual cares about dating activities *per se*. There are some fellows and girls whose interests and values are such that dating is not the only thing that matters. These individuals may deliberately limit their dating so that it doesn't interfere seriously with their other interests in life.

THE QUESTION OF HOURS

Young people, as well as those who are responsible for them, are deeply concerned about what time they should return from a date.

Why Teen-agers Stay Out Too Late

People stay out late because they're having such fun. They think that the longer the date is prolonged, the more fun they'll have. What they fail to realize is that a date may prove *less* exciting as time goes on. It's better to end any social activity while it's still at a peak than to wait until it fizzles out.

Some young people fail to recognize this need to limit themselves. Throughout life we all face limits to our freedom. If we fail to respect these limits in adolescence, we will have even greater difficulty later in life. Recognizing where individual freedom starts and ends is a mark of maturity.

Sometimes, oddly enough, teen-agers stay out later than is sensible, not because they are really having fun, but in an effort to prove to themselves that they are having fun. If you're not happy on a date, you may try to prolong it in a desperate attempt to salvage some fun. Usually this effort is unsuccessful; it would be better to end this date and plan your next one so that it's more satisfying.

How Late Is Too Late?

When should a fellow bring a girl home from a date? Who decides what time a date should end? These are typical questions asked by boys and girls—and their parents.

There is no magic time by which all dates should end. The Cinderella story with its midnight curfew makes dramatic telling, but it doesn't make much sense in real life. For some dates, midnight would be too late; for others, it would be too early. How late a date should end depends on many factors, such as:

—how old the two people are (younger individuals get in earlier)
—how responsible the couple is (the more responsible, the more leeway)
—how the parents feel about the hour question (strict or lenient)

—where the date takes place (a neighborhood movie or a distant dance)

—who else is going with the dating pair (the more to be picked up and taken home, the later)

—what time the activity will be over (no one expects to leave long before the end)

—how long it will take to be served some refreshment (is "The Greasy Spoon" always crowded after a game?)

—how far the couple has to travel to get the girl home (the farther, the later)

—what is generally considered a reasonable hour in the community

Curfew Conversations

With at least nine factors determining the lateness of a date, it's hard to find any *one* definite homecoming hour to suit all dates. Therefore, many girls find that they need to discuss each date with their parents. Then they can weigh the different factors involved.

While Jane is helping to set the table, she talks over her date plans with her mother, and together they agree on a reasonable time for Jack to get Jane home. This is decided on in the light of the kind of date it is, the confidence the parents have in their daughter and her date, and their realistic estimate of the hour by which the date should be over. If the hour is later than Jane's dad feels is sensible, then Jane and her mother may need to interpret to him just why this particular date will take so long. Most fathers are reasonable if they understand the factors involved. They get excited when they fear that their children are "chasing around" in an irresponsible way too late at night.

Clearing with the Boy

The hour question is further clarified when Jack comes to call for Jane. Of course, she invites him in for a casual chat with her folks before they start off on their date. At that time Jane may say something to this effect to her boy friend: "Jack, I told the folks that we'd probably be home by eleven o'clock. Does that seem right to you?" Or she might turn to her date and say to him, "Jack, what time shall we tell my parents to expect me home tonight?"

Either way, Jane is letting her date realize that her parents are concerned about her homecoming, and that she is taking some of the responsibility for getting home at a reasonable time. This not only reassures Jane's parents, but it may make Jack feel easier too. Some boys complain that they don't know

when their girls expect to get home, and that often they feel they have to stay out longer than they prefer because the girl seems to have no clear-cut time in mind. A fellow who has to get up early to go to work will not long appreciate missing out on his sleep. Eventually, he will just have to tell his girl that he has to work the next morning and that he is taking her home early. A sensible girl will understand his position and co-operate with him.

When young people themselves take responsibility for keeping reasonable hours, they avoid the embarrassment of parental scenes when they get home too late. If a girl wants to circumvent a trying episode, with her father treating her like a little girl, she should act adult enough to return home as promised. If teen-agers themselves assume the responsibility for getting home at a reasonable time, parents will not have to take over and make a couple feel like "a pair of kids."

A Community Understanding

One of the things that makes the hour question difficult is that some young people are allowed out until all hours and others are carefully supervised.

A girl may complain to her parents that "all the other kids stay out much later," when actually only a few have this much latitude. Neither she nor her parents really know how late other young people are allowed to stay out. The only way to answer such a question is through some collective action in which the various interested persons in a given neighborhood get together and determine a reasonable homecoming time.

Many communities are developing just such agreements. Groups of parents, teachers, and young people get together at an arranged time and decide at what hour a ninth-grade party should be over. They arrive at reasonable standards for all the other grades. Not everyone will abide by such decisions, that's true. But if everyone concerned knows, in general, what to expect, then school, church, and private affairs can be planned to terminate in conformity with the community code. Responsible young people generally try to do what is expected of them, and so this kind of code is usually honored.

THE SENIOR PROM

Some high schools have established the pattern of a great big wonderful senior prom that students "will remember for the rest of their lives." Some of these proms are planned to end officially around midnight or a little later. Then frequently, seniors drive across the county to an exciting spot for food and dancing or entertainment and prolong the evening as long as possible. In some communities the all-night prom has become a tradition.

The All-Night Prom

The all-night prom can be a gala event, or it can be a nightmare. The difference lies in how well it has been planned and how responsibly it is carried through. If it's not well organized, it may get into the hands of the most scatterbrained members of the class, who then use it as an opportunity to drive recklessly, drink, carouse, and destroy property as well as their reputations. The wild night ends up as anything but a pleasant memory.

If the all-night prom night is planned in detail by those who want young people to have a good time, it can be a huge success. In some towns one of the men's service clubs offers to work with the senior class in programing the night's entertainment. There are various possibilities for safe fun: They can all go on to a community hall for a series of acts with imported name entertainers as well as local talent. There may be a splash party at the pool. Sometimes a bowling match is scheduled for part of the night. Or folk dancing follows an evening of ballroom dancing. Whatever the activities, they are planned well ahead of time, with responsibilities allocated for keeping the fun rolling rather than degenerating.

The all-night prom usually ends with a big breakfast before everyone goes yawning home to bed. In one town, the church women got up at four in the morning to prepare sausage and pancakes for seniors as the grand climax to their night of fun. The ladies of the church preferred this to having their teen-agers roam the county roads late at night looking for a place to eat.

Planning the Prom

Planning the senior prom should be the responsibility of the seniors themselves. Adults may help, but they should not take the party away from the young people if it's to be a success. Seniors and adults in charge have a responsibility to plan the kind of party that will be of interest to every member of the class. If, for instance, there are some boys and girls who don't enjoy dancing, alternative activities should be provided. Otherwise only certain members of the class get to enjoy what all are entitled to; and there's a danger then of the bored guests wandering off into the night in search of fun elsewhere.

In any given community where the senior prom is up for discussion, the questions of how long it should last and what activities shall be included must be tackled. Finding and eliciting the help of interested men and women is the first step in attempting to broaden the scope of the senior prom. With their help, and with the permission of school authorities, the whole town will welcome the affair. But without the encouragement, assistance, and supervision of respected and respectable adults, the after-prom activities may turn out to be a great disappointment or a community headache.

WHAT MAKES THE DIFFERENCE

Late hours are not the only problem in dating. One group of kids may stay up all night singing around the piano or folk dancing at the community center and have a wonderful time. Another group may be home before midnight, but with memories that shame and burn the rest of their lives. The difference is not in the hours that were kept, but in what happened and how the persons involved felt about it.

Hours that young people keep are important—for their reputations, if for nothing else. Other people besides the dating pair are concerned with late dates. Teachers have a right to be disturbed if students fail to keep up in their work. Neighbors are usually critical. Parents certainly have an interest in their children's activities and hours. It is a concern for teen-agers too. For the youngster who is not having much fun is usually the one trying to prolong the evening in a desperate effort to make it a good time. If he gets too far out of line, he may give the whole crowd a black eye in the community.

SUMMING UP

Fellows and girls who want to earn and keep good reputations get home at reasonable hours. They recognize that the adults responsible for them have a right to know where they are going and what time they may be expected home, and they then make a real effort to get back as per agreement. A telephone call home in case of emergency will take care of an unexpected delay and secure help if it is needed. Otherwise getting home at a reasonable hour from dates just makes good sense.

8

WHAT TO DO ON A DATE

"What shall we do tonight?" is a frequent question asked by dating couples. Teen-agers are always looking for something to do that's different, that's fun, and that won't cost too much money. Social opportunities for young people are limited in many communities, and those that are available are often not as wholesome or varied as they might be.

Even young people who live in large metropolitan areas are often concerned about what to do on a date. They may be surrounded by hundreds of possibilities and yet be unaware that they exist.

One of the responsibilities that goes with dating is knowing how to use available resources for wholesome dating. Until your interests develop and your horizons widen, you may not be fully aware of the possibilities open to you in your own neighborhood. As you become accustomed to thinking in terms of dating resources, you will become increasingly able to find ways to have a variety of satisfying dates. The next time you are faced with the question of what to do on a date, you might consider one or more of the following possibilities.

GOING TO THE MOVIES

Regardless of where you live, there probably is a movie somewhere in your vicinity. If you live in a small town or in a rural community, the selection of movies may be rather limited. If you have already seen the show, or if your partner has, or if it's not particularly worth seeing, it would be better to look for some other activity. As you become aware of other dating resources, you will find yourself going to the movies only when something especially interesting is playing. And as you become more selective, you will find yourself enjoying these choice movies much more.

Movie Manners

There is an etiquette for movie dates that both young men and women should know. Briefly it is this. While the fellow buys the tickets, the girl steps aside and looks at the stills outside to avoid the boy any embarrassment he may feel at the ticket window. Once inside, the girl follows the usher to their seats, and the fellow follows the girl. If there is no usher, the boy precedes the girl down the aisle, finds two seats, and steps aside so that the girl may be seated first; he then follows and seats himself beside her.

If the girl is wearing a coat or jacket, the fellow helps her out of it and arranges it comfortably over the back of her seat. Then he removes his outer coat and hat and scarf and either places them under his seat or holds them in his lap.

During the film, the two people enjoy the picture without annoying those seated near them. Loud talking, whistling, giggling, calling across to other couples, is kid stuff. Similarly, throwing popcorn or paper, and otherwise behaving like a nuisance, is rude and crude. It may lead to your being asked to leave the theater. Expressing more familiarity than is suitable for a public place is apt to annoy people seated near you, and may be embarrassing for your date.

In many theaters there is an intermission when refreshments may be purchased. At that time the boy may ask his date what she would like, and then excuse himself while he gets it. (Sometimes refreshments may be purchased before a couple go to their seats.) If his budget doesn't call for this extra, a boy should come prepared with some little offering to take the place of the purchased refreshments, such as a candy from a roll of mints or a stick of gum. The girl accepts the offer graciously without hinting that she would like something else. As the guest of the occasion, the girl waits for her host to make the overture. It's also all right for the girl to open her purse and offer him some simple little morsel, but she shouldn't make a production of it.

The boy may hold the girl's hand if she has no objection, or place his arm over the back of her seat. Such actions do not go beyond socially acceptable behavior. They may whisper their reactions to the picture or comment to each other about the characters or the plot, so long as they neither embarrass each other nor annoy their neighbors.

When the movie is over, the boy helps the girl into her wraps, and waits in the aisle until the girl emerges and precedes him out of the theater. Then, the boy may suggest stopping at a soda fountain, if he wishes, or if it's early, the girl may invite him to her home for "cake and milk" or whatever she and her family have agreed upon for an evening snack.

How about Drive-Ins?

Going to a drive-in theater poses a somewhat different problem than going to a regular movie. Whereas almost everyone approves of young people attending movies together, behavior at drive-ins is viewed with suspicion and outright disapproval by many adults and young people. The difference lies in the extreme privacy available at the drive-in—a privilege that some couples take advantage of with irresponsible behavior. In some places, drive-ins have such an unsavory reputation that they are known as "passion pits," a designation that reflects the general recognition of what goes on in some of the cars.

Going to a drive-in movie can be a real hazard for a girl who is out with a boy she does not know well. He may turn out to want more than she should consent to. Because the couple have complete responsibility for their behavior together at a drive-in, a girl has to be relatively sure that she can trust her date. This can be ensured by going to a drive-in only with a date you know. Two people who know from experience together what they can expect of each other can enjoy the opportunity for private conversation which the drive-in movie offers, without abusing the privilege.

Parents and school and college authorities are apt to disapprove of drive-in patronage on the part of their young people for understandable reasons. If they rule against it, young couples will have to comply, unless they're out to defy authority. If adults can be given some assurance of a safe situation by the presence of older persons in the car, or by their confidence in the integrity of their children and the dating partners involved, they may possibly allow drive-in viewing.

Double dating may be a protection, but it may also add to the problem. If the other couple go in for more intimacy than you feel is appropriate, you may be in for a miserable evening. But if the other couple share your standards of conduct, their presence is a real advantage.

ENJOYING SPORTS

Whether you live in the country or in town, there are interesting sporting events somewhere nearby. Ball games of all sorts, skating, tennis, golf, bowling, and swimming all are date possibilities. Whether you're interested in spectator sports, or the "do it yourself" variety, you'll find sports increasingly rewarding. Maybe you're fortunate enough to have a professional team nearby. Have you ever seen a big league hockey game? Have you attended a college football game recently? How about your high school  basketball games? Such spectator sports are fun and usually not expensive.

Often it's more fun for you to play than to watch a game. Tennis, swimming, and skating, as well as many other sports, are good dating activities. Perhaps your date would be willing to help you learn more about some sport in which he is particularly active. Stop and look around you! What sporting opportunities are available in your neighborhood?

SCHOOL AFFAIRS

School events can be especially rewarding date experiences. Many teen-agers have great fun at school dances, parties, and other functions. If your date goes to a different school, he will probably enjoy getting into a new campus atmosphere for a change. It might even mean a return invitation for you to his school and the possibility of new contacts. If your school seems lacking in social functions, then maybe it needs a little prodding from people just like you. Perhaps there is a social committee you could join. Remember, school is run for *you,* and you can (and should) help it develop a social program that will be popular and interesting to all.

CHURCH PROGRAMS

Does your church have a youth group? If so, you have probably already experienced some good times there. Maybe your date will enjoy going to the youth meetings with you. If you enjoy them, why shouldn't he? Don't forget that enthusiasm is contagious. Even if you're dating someone of a different religion, he may be interested in attending your youth group with you. Then on your next date you might visit his.

What if your church has no youth group? Then you might want to talk with your religious leader about helping you start a group. Maybe some friends from your Sunday school class would like to get together and discuss the formation of such a group. You could plan a varied program of the kind you know would interest young people. As your group gets started, you may find that you are drawing back into the church those teen-agers and young adults who felt they had to look elsewhere for entertainment.

COMMUNITY ACTIVITIES

What youth-serving organizations are in your community that could provide dating fun? Is there a Y nearby? What type of program does your local community center have? The 4-H, Grange, FFA, and FHA programs often offer rural youth opportunities for dates. In cities there are many places offering entertainment at little or no cost which too often are overlooked. For instance, can you recall the last time you visited the local museum? Or went to the zoo? You may find them even more enjoyable now than when you were a child. A little detective work may turn up many other unusual and stimulating opportunities in types of dates right in your own backyard.

HOBBIES AND INTERESTS

A large number of young people don't have to wonder what to do when they're together because they're already engrossed in mutually absorbing activities. Young people who belong to an orchestra, band, choral group, or Hi-Fi club find enjoyment together in practicing, getting ready for concerts, going to other musical events, and generally exploring together the wide, wide world of music. For the young person who has had few opportunities to develop musical talents, it's never too late. He can always join a beginners' group or course or take private lessons. Such activities not only bring a sense of personal accomplishment but also lead to acquaintance with other persons who find joy in music.

Belonging to a drama group offers rich opportunity for enjoying others and trying out your abilities in a variety of situations. You find out if you have talent in acting, or in designing scenery or costumes. Maybe you turn out to be a lighting expert. Interest grows with experience, and you will find yourself becoming more aware of the special spell of the theater and enjoying plays more and more with your new associates.

In fact, all hobby groups are rewarding. Young people who belong to a camera or craft club, a nature or hiking group, find that they not only enjoy their interests together and learn a lot about them, but also get to know one another. When they get together over hobbies, it can be as much fun as a more formal date.

It's safe to say that the girl who does things goes places. As she increases the number and variety of her interests, she increases the number of people she knows and enjoys. As a result, she gets invited to more and more activities taking place within the interest group, and also on dates with individual members of the group. The same holds true for a young man. As he matures and discovers talents along a number of lines, his world expands, his acquaintances multiply, and he finds himself at home with an increasing number of groups and individuals. There is nothing quite like getting out of yourself and into activities and interests that can be shared with others.

FUN AT HOME

Many teen-agers who complain that "there's nothing to do on dates" overlook their own homes. There are countless ways of turning your home into a happy dating place for yourself and your friends.

Your parents, as well as your friends, will probably be glad to help you with the planning. Why not *give* a party, for a change? Playing the host can be fun if you approach it with a little imagination. Your radio or record player can provide the music for dancing. Party books and articles will introduce you to novel games. Your friends will pitch in to help supply refreshments—and even records.

Making your parties a little different is a sure way to make them successful. You may tire of parties where you only dance and eat. But if you put a little time into *planning* a party, your guests may rate you host of the year. Your library carries books on party preparation which are full of novel ideas. The idea is to give a party with a "theme." How about a scavenger or treasure hunt? Or you could plan a progressive party in which you go to each guest's house for another refreshment and another activity. Holiday parties are always festive—so are celebrations after school football victories.

It Need Not Be a Party

What else can you do at home besides throw a party? Maybe your parents have saved the records they collected in their younger days. Your friends may enjoy hearing these quaint discs as much as you do. Maybe there's an old-fashioned ice cream freezer in your attic. It might be fun to get some cracked ice and other makings and freeze ice cream yourself. Is there also a trunk full of old clothes there? Then how about playing charades or improvising an old melodrama? An old table in the basement might suggest an evening of crafts. Imagination, innovation, and a willingness to suggest activities that your friends might enjoy make for good times together.

Young people who live in apartments also have many fun-filled opportunities at hand. Most boys and girls love to cook. Why not try your hand at making some foreign dish? An old-fashioned taffy pull lends itself to hilarious, if sticky, informality. You might even like to prepare a simple meal together. It's fun to work and plan together, especially if you are carrying out your own ideas. And think of how your date's eyes will glow when your parents compliment him on the pizza he made! Whether you plan your evening at home for twenty, or just for two, it can be one of the nicest dates you've ever had.

WHAT TO TALK ABOUT ON A DATE

Carrying on a pleasant conversation on a date need not be the torment that many inexperienced young people fear. The boy who talks about his interests and encourages his girl to talk about hers won't have time to worry about conversation —he'll be making it! The girl who cultivates the art of listening as well as talking and gives her date undivided attention will never seem like a dull companion.

The general principle is: Talk about your likes and interests on a date. What specifically could some of these appropriate topics be?

> Activities in the community, on the campus, or at school
> Current sports events
> News stories of popular interest
> Personal experiences and plans
> Prevalent fun-talk (riddles, "slanguage," anecdotes, jokes, puns)

If you feel inadequate about conversation, you may want to go through such magazines as *Reader's Digest, Coronet, Pageant, Compact,* or some similar resource for amusing and interesting stories that might be shared on the date. As you get more and more experience, you won't need to prepare yourself so specifically. You will be able to suit your talk to the mood of the moment and use your own resources for being pleasant, entertaining, and at ease.

You should express your feelings on a date, as well as your interests. The girl who says, "I feel so happy dancing with you," is sharing with her escort a mood that is important to both of them. The boy who brings his date to her door saying, "You've made me feel wonderful tonight," does much more than just say he had a good time. He lets her know that she is something special. Spontaneity adds charm to a personality as well as to a relationship.

GETTING ACQUAINTED

If this is the first time you are taking a certain girl out, it's a good idea to plan an activity that will give you a chance to know her better. At the same time it will be easier if you don't put yourself into a position conducive to awkward silences. Especially if you feel insecure with your new date, it helps to plan something that won't depend entirely on your ability as a conversationalist.

If you are taking her to the movies, try to arrange for a few minutes before or after to get acquainted. If the movie is not too far away, you might walk there. This will give you a chance to talk together, and any silence that does come up won't seem quite as deadly in this situation. Perhaps there's a ball game coming up at school. If she would consent to go with you, it might serve as a talking point until you feel more at ease with her. Maybe a mutual friend is giving a party. If you take her there on the first date, you will be with friends whom you both know and neither of you will feel too ill at ease.

When you are deciding where to go on the first date, it's a good idea to get some notion of the kinds of things this girl likes to do. If you are walking her home after school, you might express your interest in baseball and see if she responds before you issue an invitation to a game. Maybe she is fascinated by some particular movie star. Inviting her to a movie in which he appears would be a good start.

Keeping Dates Interesting

The more you go out with a girl, the more trouble you may have finding new and different things to do. If you get into the habit of going to the same place every time, you may find yourselves losing interest in the place and perhaps in each other. So try to plan for something new and different the next time you go out. What have you especially enjoyed doing in the past? What opportunities are available that you haven't tapped? It's your job to keep your dates interesting if you want to keep your date interested.

Double and Triple Dates

You may want to double date with another couple—or with two or three other couples. In such a case the decision on what to do is not yours alone. Everyone involved will want to have some part in deciding where you go and what you do. Regardless of how much you want to attend a particular place, you may be outvoted. Someone may have seen the movie you suggest or have gone bowling only last night.

If you're spending the evening with other couples, it's best to plan something that will give you all a chance to become better acquainted. Barbecues, picnics at the park, and trips to local places of interest are often more fun in a group. There is no point to a double date if each couple keeps exclusively to themselves. So try to plan things that will involve everyone and that everyone involved will enjoy.

Steady Dates

If you're going steady, you should be even more eager to keep your dates interesting. By now you have probably gotten to the point where your date helps decide what you're going to do. A regular Saturday night date need not become routine and ordinary. In addition to the movies and evenings at home, plan something special once in a while. This doesn't have to cost a lot of money. You and your steady might visit a nearby flower show, a bird sanctuary, or a museum. You might take an afternoon hike, or a bicycle trip to explore nearby surroundings. Walking and talking, or singing together, are excellent ways of getting to know each other better. You might like to guess about the people you see, or make up stories about houses and scenery on the way.

You and your steady date should be at the point where conversation comes easily. Having occasional dates which provide the opportunity for long talks will lead to even further understanding.

WHOSE DECISION IS IT?

Does the boy always decide what's to be done on a date? Most boys will admit that the answer is "No." In fact, many complain that their dates give them little chance at suggestions about date activities. What to do on a date can be a real cause of friction between a couple. Maybe a hockey

game is in town, and the girl insists on going to a movie. If the boy wins the argument, the girl may spoil his evening by pouting and complaining. If the boy gives in to the girl, he might withdraw into his shell and be a bore all evening. Who should make the decision?

Usually if you and your date discuss the various possibilities, you can reach a decision that will please both of you. If, however, either of you approaches the discussion with your mind already made up, it can prove difficult. There are many things to consider when deciding where to go. You will want to ask yourself how important it is to your date to do what she wants. It's not wise to insist on having your own way to prove that you can do it. Your date will only resent it. If you each try to see the other's point of view, you can reach a mutually satisfying decision more easily.

Ask yourself if you can put off your preference to another time. Maybe the hockey game is in town only tonight, whereas the movie will be playing through all next week. It would be the logical and mature thing to realize that the game is probably very important to your date or he wouldn't be insisting on seeing it. So why not plan on the movies for the following date?

Any mature decision is made co-operatively between the persons involved. The decision can also be of concern to the parents, or dorm mother, as well as to the couple. As you go further and further into dating, you will learn to recognize the invitations that are generally approved, and those that you had better decline.

Whatever you decide to do, the important thing is how you decided. If you both had a part in the decision, after reaching an understanding you both have a satisfying feeling. Consideration of another person's values and desires and a willingness to talk things over leads to a mature understanding.

PERSONAL APPEARANCE ON A DATE

The way you look on a date is important. In a nationwide poll of thousands of teen-agers, Dr. Christensen found that when both boys and girls listed what they considered important in making or accepting dates, "pride in personal appearance and manners" ranked third. This doesn't mean that a girl has to be a beauty queen or that a boy must be handsome. It does mean that both sexes expect a date to make an acceptable appearance and behave in a socially acceptable manner.

Dress Appropriately

There is a fashion etiquette as well as a movie or eating etiquette. Dressing to suit the occasion is part of fashion knowhow. You will feel silly in high heels at the basketball game if the other girls are wearing saddle shoes. Your date may resent having to help you up and down the stands continually so that you don't fall. To a sports event you should wear casual clothes, just as to most parties you should wear dressy clothes.

When your date invites you out, he may give you some indication of the type of dress which would be appropriate. If he doesn't, it's perfectly acceptable to ask a boy if this is to be a casual sweater-and-skirt affair, a dress-up or a really gala formal affair. If he tells you what he's wearing it may give you some indication of what outfit you should choose. Girls going to the same event frequently clear with each other on what they will wear.

Boys, too, need to dress appropriately. You will look and feel out of place if the other boys are in sport shirts and you are wearing your best suit. You might be embarrassed if you show up for a party in Levi's and find your date wearing a fancy dress. The best thing is to check with your date ahead of time about clothes. Find out what is expected of you, and let her know what is expected of her.

Neatness Does It

Regardless of what you wear, you want to be well groomed. A handsome suit will be wasted if your nails are dirty and your hair uncombed. A girl may manage to look attractive in an old skirt and blouse because she's neat and well groomed. But even the most beautiful girl looks unattractive if she's grimy.

When young people all over the country talk about what they consider important in a date, cleanliness and neatness rank high. Girls are not as interested in fellows who show up for dates with dirty T-shirts or uncombed hair. No boy wants to escort a girl who is sloppy. Recently the young men on one college campus openly revolted against the trend among certain coeds to appear unkempt. They protested that they wanted girls to look feminine. Certainly this isn't too much to expect of a date.

ENJOYING A DATE

You and your date have mutually decided where you are going. You have taken care to be dressed appropriately. You have taken pains to be clean and neat. But even these precautions don't insure success on a date. A date is wholly satisfying only when each person is considerate of the other. Dating is not fun if either of you:

—flirts conspicuously with others
—brags about previous conquests
—gossips about other dates
—clings too closely to members of your own sex
—avoids participation in the activities
—makes an issue over minor mishaps

Such behavior is essentially a lack of courtesy, and it can really keep you from enjoying each other. Often one or more of these breaches of etiquette can lose you a second date with your escort.

Courtesy Is More Than Manners

It may seem out of place to bring up courtesy here. You may feel that, of course, you are naturally courteous to all your acquaintances. But it might be a good idea to take stock of yourself to see just how courteous you really are. Mary, when was the last time you thanked your date as he held the door for you? John, when was the last time you helped your date out of the car instead of leaving her to fend for herself? Do you always remember to thank your date's parents for "that wonderful dinner"? How often do you tell your date how much you enjoyed the evening? All of these things are just common courtesy. It seems, however, that the more we date a particular person, the more we take him or her for granted.

A fellow may say to himself, "Of course I enjoyed the date; she knows that." Yet think how good it would make her feel if he told her once in a while. How much more her parents would think of him if the boy stuck his head in the door and told them how much he enjoyed the evening. Such courtesies go a long way toward making a boy a good date and a pleasant companion.

Sincerity Is Honesty

Some boys seem to be naturally courteous. They're quite suave about giving a girl the impression that they are genuinely interested in her. Some girls fall easily for a fellow's line. They like to hear that they're beautiful, wonderful, and first in his heart. If a fellow is genuinely friendly and likes a girl, he doesn't need a "line" to make her believe it. He can show her in his manner that he likes her. Many girls are leery of boys who "pour it on." They steer clear of boys who tell all the girls the same thing.

Kidding, punning, flattering, and teasing all are fun on a date when both the fellow and the girl recognize what game it is they are playing, and when they mutually enjoy it. When it is exploitive or one-sided, usually one person is being amused at the expense of the other.

Sincerity is an attractive quality. If you feel your date hitting close to home when she says, "I'll bet you tell that to all the girls," now is the time to reconsider. In feeding a line you're not only "buttering up" the girl, you're not being honest with yourself. Girls also want to be careful to say what they mean, and mean what they say. If you are dishonest about one thing, your date may get the feeling that you can't be trusted at all. But if you are sincere in what you tell your date, your whole relationship will be on a higher plane.

Being Yourself

Girls are sometimes accused of putting on an act when they're out on a date. Boys are not favorably impressed when a girl tries to act sophisticated or put on airs. Neither are girls pleased by boys who strut and brag and pretend to be more than they are.

We often feel the need to put on airs because we're unsure of ourselves. If we act naturally, we may find that people like us as we are, and our feelings of inferiority will diminish.

Wherever you go, whatever you do, whoever you are, try to relax and be yourself. Your richest satisfaction comes when you realize that your date and others accept you as **you** really are.

HOW MUCH DO DATES COST?

As soon as you enter your teens you start to be concerned about money. For the first few years of life, your needs are pretty well taken care of by your parents. If you want something you ask them to buy it for you or to give you the money for it. You're more concerned about whether or not you can have something than where the money will come from for it. To some youngsters, parents seem to have an endless supply of money. Other children are given a part from a very young age in making family decisions about the spending of money. Regardless of what type of upbringing you have, in high school and college you probably have money problems. No matter how much money you get, it never seems to be enough.

Dr. Martin Bloom recently conducted a study of the money problems of 1,973 students from the 7th through the 12th grades. He found that "adolescents are very much concerned with the problem of obtaining money." He reports that many of the adolescents he interviewed "had difficulty in keeping up with school expenses and personal grooming, and feel embarrassed because of lack of funds." Dr. Bloom found that 10th-graders have the most money worries of all, but that older youth have money problems too. Many teen-agers wish that their school would give them more help with their personal financial problems. Some schools have banks that train students to develop a regular saving program for things that are important to them.

Students need money for many things. They often must provide for their own books and school expenses. They need money for school lunches and for after-school refreshments. Many teen-agers buy their own clothes and pay for practically all their own personal expenses. Most of all, dating takes up a major portion of the allowances of many young adults.

129

THE BOY PAYS . . .

Sometimes boys seem to spend a large proportion of their money on dating expenses. Many young men continually worry about where the money will come from for their next date. What if the girl wants to spend more than he can afford?

Actually, dates do not have to be more expensive than the boy can afford. What are some of the expenses the average young man has when he dates?

For Transportation

When a young man dates, the cost of transportation looms large. If he uses the family car, he is responsible for putting in gas and oil. If it's his own car, he also may have to cover such expenses as repairs, maintenance, and insurance. He must either wash the car himself or pay to have it washed. Using a car is convenient but it's not cheap.

If a fellow doesn't have use of a car, he must use public transportation to and from his date's home. If he's within walking distance of her home, he still must pay transportation if they go out together. When she wears a formal, he feels that he must use a taxi to take her to and from the dance. If the couple picks places close enough to walk to, the expense will not be as great, but this is not always possible or even advisable.

For Entertainment

Dating expenses just begin with transportation. The young man must almost always pay for entertainment on the date. At the movies he pays the admission charge. Most dances have entrance fees. Even many sports events at school cost money. Sometimes it's hard to find activities that are not too expensive.

For Food

Mothers often remark that teen-agers seem to have a bottomless pit for a stomach. They are always hungry. Who knows this better than the teen-agers themselves who have to pay for the food consumed on dates? It's not always possible to go home and raid the refrigerator after a date. Boys need money to buy Cokes for their dates and themselves after school. They want money to purchase popcorn and candy at the movies. Then after a movie or dance they often feel they must have money to suggest a hamburger or a malted. Every time his date says she is hungry, another large bite comes out of a boy's allowance.

For Clothes and Grooming

Looking nice costs money also. The expenses incurred while dating must include money spent for clothes and grooming. Do you have to pay for having your suit cleaned before the next dance? What about shaving cream and deodorant? You may need to rent a tuxedo for the big prom. Did you have your hair cut before your last date? All of these expenses mount up.

THE GIRL SPENDS . . .

Some boys are amazed to hear that their dates also have money problems. They ask, "Why do girls need money? We pay all the dating expenses!" But actually, girls do have considerable expense when they go out with boys.

For Clothes

A boy can get by with one good suit. Wearing this suit with different shirts is all he really needs for almost any function that may come up. For many events a sport shirt and slacks is adequate.

Girls need many more clothes. Almost every girl would feel badly if she had only one dress to wear to every event. She wants a selection of dresses to choose from. Girls also need a larger variety of clothes than boys do. They need slacks or Bermudas for very informal occasions. They need blouses and skirts for weekday dates. They need "dressy" dresses for parties, and a formal for the big prom. Since girls' sizes vary so much, it's not always easy to borrow clothes from friends and relatives, although this is done sometimes for special occasions.

For Grooming

Girls usually need more money than boys do for grooming. Unless a girl sets her own hair she needs money for the beauty parlor. Even if she gives herself a home permanent

she needs money for supplies. Girls are likely to use more expensive shampoos and face creams. Make-up is a constant expense. In general, the cost of keeping a girl looking attractive is more than that of keeping a boy looking neat.

For Parties

Parties are more frequently given by girls than boys. Often the girl has to pay out of her allowance for the refreshments, games, and records. Although these parties may not occur as frequently as dates for which the boy pays, they generally cost more money than a regular date. When a boy takes out a girl he pays only for two. When a girl gives a party, she usually invites several other couples. Food costs alone can be great if she plans extensive refreshments.

HOW MUCH TO SPEND?

No one can tell you how much you *should* spend for a date. That is something you will have to decide in view of your entire situation. It may help to know what other teen-agers *do* spend for dates. The range is wide. Some dates cost nothing, and some cost quite a lot of money. One fellow (formerly a member of the armed forces) reported that he once spent $300 on one date!

Dr. Ruth Connor and Edith Flinn Hall did a study on dating expenses of freshman and sophomore college students. They report that college students spend "$2 to $3 for routine dates, $5 to $6 for special dates, and $20 to $35 for big affairs." A high school prom or college homecoming can be very expensive.

It's a good idea to budget your date money so that you have enough money when the big prom comes up. Maybe for several weeks before the prom you can plan less expensive dates and save a little. If you explain the situation to your girl, she is usually willing to co-operate. After all, it's a big event for her too, and she would like you to be able to handle it graciously.

WHERE DOES THE MONEY COME FROM?

With all of the expenses a teen-ager incurs he must have some regular source of income. It may help to know some of the different ways in which teen-agers get money.

Ask-As-You-Need Plan

Some youngsters get along asking for money as the need for it arises. But this isn't completely satisfactory for either the teen-ager or the adult. Teen-agers *need* some money to call their own. They want to be able to get money without having to give elaborate explanations of what they plan to do with it. They dread the parental question, "What do you want it for this time?"

Young adults resent having to ask for every cent they need. Besides, this keeps them from developing a real responsibility for money. If they consider their mother or father as an endless supply of money, they never will learn how to budget their own money carefully. Then, when they marry, they may find that they are not capable of handling their finances.

This arrangement is not very satisfactory to parents either. They may feel they need to know what's being done with the money they hand out, but it probably would make them feel even better if just one night they weren't being asked for money. Some fathers get the feeling that they are loved only for their handouts. They may not seem to realize that teen-agers don't like asking for money any more than they like being asked.

Getting an Allowance

Allowances seem to be a good way of distributing the family income. Mother decides how much she needs to run the house. Father decides how much he needs to meet his expenses. The children all decide how much they really need for themselves. Then in family discussion the family decides together who is to get how much and for what. Most teen-agers find that having an allowance gives them a feeling of independence. They have some money that they can spend as they wish, without accounting for every cent. Even if they feel that their allowances are too small, they still prefer having money they can call their own.

Parents, too, usually favor this arrangement. This way they're not continually pestered for money, and they can feel some assurance that their son or daughter will develop responsibility for living within the allowance. Occasionally special events come up that require an "advance," but parents can help a teen-ager learn to plan for such events so that "advances" are not so frequent.

If a teen-ager just can't seem to stay within his allowance, it might be wise for him to discuss it with his parents. Maybe his expenses are really greater than the allowance provides for. Perhaps the family budget can be stretched a little to help with these needs. Maybe the young person should get a part-time job to supplement his income. Regardless of what is decided, the important thing is that it was decided together.

Working at Home

Some teen-agers work at home to earn money. They take stock of jobs around the house that need to be done and suggest an earning plan. Boys can contract to mow the lawn, help in the garden, clean the attic, or shovel snow to earn money. Girls may help with the house cleaning, dishwashing, cooking, and sewing. If your father has his car washed at the

garage, maybe he would be willing to have you wash it instead. If you did a good enough job, perhaps he would make it a permanent arrangement. If your mother usually hires someone to wash her windows, perhaps she would be willing to let you show her that you can do them just as well. Working at home, with or without pay, helps prepare young adults for their own futures as homemakers.

Part-Time Jobs

When the family budget cannot stretch far enough to include all that teen-agers feel they need, a part-time job will help. Paper boys, part-time clerks, baby sitters, and fountain clerks are often young adults who are helping supplement their income by working part time. Teen-agers can discuss the situation thoroughly with their parents before obtaining part-time work. Such questions as, "Will your work fit in with your schedule?" and "Will it allow enough time for school work and home responsibilities?" have to be answered realistically.

Teen-agers get a feeling of independence from working outside the home. They like to feel that they're earning their own money rather than accepting it from the family. Sometimes they contribute some of their earnings to the family or have their parents save some for their future. Part-time jobs can be a big help if you need money, just so long as they don't cut into your school and home activities too much.

Cutting Dating Expenses

If you have exhausted every possible source of money and you still don't have enough, then maybe you must cut down on your dating expenses. The next time you go to the movies, try walking instead of taking the bus. Not only will it save you money but you may find that it's a good opportunity to talk to your date and get to know her. Instead of that expensive movie in the next town, why not see the one closer home? Or a movie on television may be better than the one you're going to pay to see.

You could cut down on expenses for a big prom by planning a party after the dance (with your friends) instead of going to a fancy night club in the city. By saving a bit here and a bit there, you'll find that your date expenses can be cut considerably.

Avoid Embarrassment

Most girls understand if you don't have a lot of money. They realize what expense a date entails and don't expect elaborate plans every time. There are ways of letting a girl know that you can't afford the most expensive thing on the menu. If you are at a restaurant after a dance and your money is getting low, suggest some low-priced item that you know she likes. Don't risk the chance of her ordering more than you can afford. She can't know how much your budget can swing unless you give her some indication.

Perhaps you could look at the menu and say, "The cherry cokes are very good here," or, "What kind of sandwich would you like?" That way she will realize that your finances indicate something around that price range. If she doesn't catch on, you may just have to tell her that money is a bit tight tonight.

A girl on a date often has difficulty figuring out just how much a boy has to spend. She is as anxious as he is to keep out of embarrassing situations. If he doesn't come forth with suggestions within his price range, she can ask what he's going to have. His order will give her some indication of the amount of money he plans to spend.

When planning what to do on a date, a girl should be considerate of the boy's wallet. Instead of automatically suggesting something rather expensive, she might offer several possibilities so that he can pick the one most suitable to his pocket.

GOING DUTCH

Some girls are quite willing to pay part of the expenses on special dates. When something is planned which is beyond the boy's means, a girl may suggest that she pay her share. Dutch-treat dates, once in a while, can be a great help to a boy.

The Purdue Opinion Panel 1957 Poll of 10,000 high school students finds that the popularity of "going Dutch" is declining among teen-agers. In 1948, 37 per cent thought that boys and girls sharing expenses "fifty-fifty" was a good idea. By 1957, only 25 per cent favored the practice. Boys now have more money than they did in 1948, and in most cases they like to pay their full dating costs.

Many young people would prefer to have a girl help out in other ways than by going Dutch. They enjoy the parties she gives, the special events she arranges, or occasionally a date at her home watching television, for instance. Whether or not you Dutch-date depends on how you and your crowd feel about it.

HOW IMPORTANT IS MONEY?

One teen-age girl asks if there is any way that she can let the boy she's dating know that money is not important to her. She would much rather have an at-home date, dancing or making candy, than not see him at all just because he doesn't have the money. Many girls feel this way. When you get right down to it, money is not the most important factor for creating a good time. If you and your date enjoy just being together, it really doesn't matter if you are going for a walk or sitting in fifth-row center seats at a Broadway musical.

Of course, special events are fun occasionally. But it's not necessary to spend money every time. It might be much more fun to splurge one night and take it easy for a month or two. When you look back on some of the dates you enjoyed most, you will realize that money is not necessarily what makes for fun.

INEXPENSIVE FUN

Lack of funds need not keep you from dating. Girls understand that boys are not always financially solvent. If the U.S. Government has trouble balancing its budget, why can't you?

Here are some suggestions of things which you and your date may enjoy doing on little or no money.

Most young adults find that their schools, churches, and clubs have active programs which do not cost a great deal of money. A school play or a church social can provide an evening of fun at little expense.

Museums, art institutes, zoos, state parks and many other publicly owned places, make excellent dating excursions. If you hail from a rural area it might be fun to plan a trip sometime to the nearest city. Once there, you could visit the library, museum, and zoo. If you pack a picnic lunch you can have a whole day of fun with your date at a minimum of expense. Similarly, if you live in the city you might enjoy going out to the country for a marshmallow roast or over to a coastline town to see the piers and boats.

When the budget has stretched to the limit, there is no place like home. See page 116, Chapter 8, for suggestions on how to make at-home dates exciting. By working in co-operation with your parents, you can plan pleasant and interesting dates without spending money.

SUMMING UP

Both boys and girls have many date expenses. To some young adults it's a real problem; to others it's a challenge—how can they make their dates both interesting and inexpensive? Dates cost anywhere from under $1 up! How much your dates cost depends upon how much you want to spend and how much imagination you use to make your dates more fun and less money. Whether you get your money from your parents or from a part-time job, you will want to plan your expenses in such a way as to allow enough for the items you must buy and the special events that come along.

If your money is limited, there are ways to earn more money or to cut down dating expenses. Your date would usually much rather do something inexpensive than go out less often and spend more money.

Money is necessary. You need it for school and grooming expenses, for gifts and even for clothes. But you do not need a lot of money to have a good time on a date.

10

CARS, DATES, AND FAMILIES

Cars are often a cause of friction between young people and their families. Sometimes parents just don't seem to realize how important a car can be to a teen-ager. And conversely, teen-agers don't understand why parents feel such anxiety and concern over their use of the family car. If most of the young men you know have access to a car, it seems even more unreasonable if you are not permitted to drive. Cars often cause problems among teen-agers themselves. If you are responsible for the family car, haven't you had the difficult experience of explaining to a friend why you can't permit him to borrow it?

A BOY AND HIS CAR

Many teen-age boys today feel keenly the need to own, or have access to, a car. Driving a car gives a boy a sense of power. It helps him feel important. He has something to show off. Many girls make a fuss over a boy who drives. A boy may feel that a girl will not date him unless he has a car. Young men who are mechanically inclined want something they can work on, take apart, and put back together. Some fellows spend hour after hour in the garage tinkering with their cars.

The Family Car

Unfortunately there is often disagreement over the use of the family car. Father may feel that you are too young to drive by yourself. Even if you are of legal age, your parents may think that you're not responsible enough to be trusted with the family car. Dad knows that the insurance rates are higher because there are more accidents among teen-age drivers. For this reason he may feel that it's too soon for you to drive. Even if you understand and agree with your parents' feelings, you may still have a longing to drive. There are so many more places you could go. Your girl seems to want to go by car, so what can you do?

Using the family car often proves more difficult than having a car of your own. Maybe your parents want to use the car the same night you do. Perhaps you have brothers and sisters who also use the car. When you feel *you* really need the car, it's hard to realize that other members of the family may also feel *they* need it. Since it's not usually possible for everyone to have his own car, some sort of compromise needs to be worked out.

To avoid the constant disagreements about who will use the family car, it's a good idea to work out arrangements ahead of time. Possibly you will each choose a definite night when you will have use of the car. As special events come up, you can request permission in advance to use the car.

Your Own Car!

While having your own car is more convenient, it means added responsibility for you. *You* must be able to assume the cost of purchase and maintenance. *You* will be the one who has to keep it in running condition. *You* are responsible for insurance, gas, and repairs. Even if you fix it yourself, you have to pay for parts.

Despite the added responsibility, owning a car may be very important to you. Your parents may not appreciate having their car "souped up" by you and your friends. If it's your

own car, you may tinker as you wish, or paint it any color you like. Also, the added prestige may be important to you.

ARE YOU READY FOR CAR DATES?

Parents are often concerned about teen-agers going on car dates too soon. And they have good reason. The fact is that some teen-agers are not prepared sufficiently for car dates. Regardless of how much you want to drive, if you are not old enough to get a license you should not risk driving a car. Here are some other things you and your parents may want to consider together.

Your Parents' Consent

You may feel that you are responsible enough to drive a car. Your parents may have a different view. The question is why? Perhaps you haven't proved yourself responsible in other ways? If your mother still has to pick up after you around the house, it's understandable if she feels you won't be responsible with a car. If you forget to come home in time for dinner, your dad may think that you'll also forget to fill the car with gas or check the oil and water. Before permitting

you prove nothing by taking chances except your unreadiness to drive at all.

Girls, too, must be psychologically ready for car dates. Before you go off on a joy ride, do you consider how well you know the driver? Will he respect your wishes about safety precautions? Do you feel you would have the courage to get out of a car if a boy threatened to drive recklessly? Your life might depend on it. It's up to a girl to let her date know that she is definitely NOT interested in watching the speedometer climb or racing another car. Without being rude, she can let the driver know that she considers unsafe driving childish. If she *cannot* convince the boy, which is rarely the case, she *can* insist that he stop the car and let her out.

SAFETY FIRST

Knowledge of the basic rules of driving safety, and being concerned about following them, is very important. When you are driving, drive. The driver's seat is no place for games, for necking, or for proving your power. You can't concentrate on other things and still be a safe driver. A girl has to keep this in mind too. If she wants to be sure of getting home that night, she shouldn't snuggle up too close while her date is driving. Distracting the driver can cause accidents. The car is a powerful machine; it can be safe or it can be deadly. It all depends on you.

Speeding Is Murder

Speeding is one of the most frequent causes of accidents. Most states designate speed limits in all areas. The speed laws tell you the maximum speed at which it is safe to drive. On dark nights, on unfamiliar roads, you will probably want

own car, you may tinker as you wish, or paint it any color you like. Also, the added prestige may be important to you.

ARE YOU READY FOR CAR DATES?

Parents are often concerned about teen-agers going on car dates too soon. And they have good reason. The fact is that some teen-agers are not prepared sufficiently for car dates. Regardless of how much you want to drive, if you are not old enough to get a license you should not risk driving a car. Here are some other things you and your parents may want to consider together.

Your Parents' Consent

You may feel that you are responsible enough to drive a car. Your parents may have a different view. The question is why? Perhaps you haven't proved yourself responsible in other ways? If your mother still has to pick up after you around the house, it's understandable if she feels you won't be responsible with a car. If you forget to come home in time for dinner, your dad may think that you'll also forget to fill the car with gas or check the oil and water. Before permitting

you prove nothing by taking chances except your unreadiness to drive at all.

Girls, too, must be psychologically ready for car dates. Before you go off on a joy ride, do you consider how well you know the driver? Will he respect your wishes about safety precautions? Do you feel you would have the courage to get out of a car if a boy threatened to drive recklessly? Your life might depend on it. It's up to a girl to let her date know that she is definitely NOT interested in watching the speedometer climb or racing another car. Without being rude, she can let the driver know that she considers unsafe driving childish. If she *cannot* convince the boy, which is rarely the case, she *can* insist that he stop the car and let her out.

SAFETY FIRST

Knowledge of the basic rules of driving safety, and being concerned about following them, is very important. When you are driving, drive. The driver's seat is no place for games, for necking, or for proving your power. You can't concentrate on other things and still be a safe driver. A girl has to keep this in mind too. If she wants to be sure of getting home that night, she shouldn't snuggle up too close while her date is driving. Distracting the driver can cause accidents. The car is a powerful machine; it can be safe or it can be deadly. It all depends on you.

Speeding Is Murder

Speeding is one of the most frequent causes of accidents. Most states designate speed limits in all areas. The speed laws tell you the maximum speed at which it is safe to drive. On dark nights, on unfamiliar roads, you will probably want

own car, you may tinker as you wish, or paint it any color you like. Also, the added prestige may be important to you.

ARE YOU READY FOR CAR DATES?

Parents are often concerned about teen-agers going on car dates too soon. And they have good reason. The fact is that some teen-agers are not prepared sufficiently for car dates. Regardless of how much you want to drive, if you are not old enough to get a license you should not risk driving a car. Here are some other things you and your parents may want to consider together.

Your Parents' Consent

You may feel that you are responsible enough to drive a car. Your parents may have a different view. The question is why? Perhaps you haven't proved yourself responsible in other ways? If your mother still has to pick up after you around the house, it's understandable if she feels you won't be responsible with a car. If you forget to come home in time for dinner, your dad may think that you'll also forget to fill the car with gas or check the oil and water. Before permitting

you to go on car dates, your parents have to be sure that you are mature enough to accept the responsibilities.

Once you have proved you can take responsibility for other things, your parents may be willing to discuss your use of the car. When you talk with your parents about using a car you may want to have clear-cut understandings about just what your responsibilities are. Who will pay for the gas? What about the increased rate in insurance? Who will be responsible for scratches or dents in the fender? Many parents feel that if they have a definite understanding about these responsibilities, the arrangement is more feasible. In some communities there is a printed agreement which both the son and father sign, designating the responsibilities each assumes. You and your father could make one up yourselves.

The same holds true for girls who want to go on car dates. When you step into a car you are just as responsible as the driver for what goes on. If your parents are convinced that both you and your date will adhere to safety rules and speed limits, they will feel better about it. It will also be up to you to get home on time so that your parents don't worry. If you're delayed, you are probably expected to do them the courtesy of calling and explaining. If your parents permit only a limited number of car dates, it is up to you to stick by that agreement. Riding around recklessly during your school lunch hour may only convince your folks that you are not ready for such dates. Often cars are filled with so many teenagers that driving becomes dangerous. You may have to realize that this chance is not worth taking.

School and College Regulations

Even if you have your parents' consent to go on car dates, it may still be forbidden on your college campus. There are very good reasons for this, and it pays to respect the rules. In this case you must limit your driving to vacations and to week ends when you're home. So far as college girls are concerned, if your campus rules against it, it's easier to say "No" to a car ride than to explain to parents and teachers why you didn't conform to school policies.

Proper Preparation

Before you undertake to drive, be sure that you are properly prepared. Have you had driving lessons from a competent instructor? Do you have knowledge of the state rules and regulations? Are you sure of what the various warning street signs mean? Many high schools and colleges offer courses in driving. These are a great help. If you are taught by a member of your family, some further research may help give you a complete understanding of what is expected of you when you drive. Driving without a license is both irresponsible and illegal. Parents and young people are wise to insist that only licensed drivers handle a car. Ignorance of the law is no excuse, as many teen-age drivers have learned to their sorrow.

The Right Attitude

No matter how great your driving skill is, you may still be far from ready to drive. Your attitude can literally mean the difference between life and death. Do you believe in driving carefully? Are you convinced that juvenile "car games" such as "chicken" are dangerous? Cars are a means of transportation; they are not toys to play with or means for showing off. The papers are filled with stories of young people who died or were seriously hurt trying to prove to their dates how fast they could drive, or trying to "outrun" the police. Actually

you prove nothing by taking chances except your unreadiness to drive at all.

Girls, too, must be psychologically ready for car dates. Before you go off on a joy ride, do you consider how well you know the driver? Will he respect your wishes about safety precautions? Do you feel you would have the courage to get out of a car if a boy threatened to drive recklessly? Your life might depend on it. It's up to a girl to let her date know that she is definitely NOT interested in watching the speedometer climb or racing another car. Without being rude, she can let the driver know that she considers unsafe driving childish. If she *cannot* convince the boy, which is rarely the case, she *can* insist that he stop the car and let her out.

SAFETY FIRST

Knowledge of the basic rules of driving safety, and being concerned about following them, is very important. When you are driving, drive. The driver's seat is no place for games, for necking, or for proving your power. You can't concentrate on other things and still be a safe driver. A girl has to keep this in mind too. If she wants to be sure of getting home that night, she shouldn't snuggle up too close while her date is driving. Distracting the driver can cause accidents. The car is a powerful machine; it can be safe or it can be deadly. It all depends on you.

Speeding Is Murder

Speeding is one of the most frequent causes of accidents. Most states designate speed limits in all areas. The speed laws tell you the maximum speed at which it is safe to drive. On dark nights, on unfamiliar roads, you will probably want

to drive considerably under the limit. Whether or not there is a speed limit, you must be extremely careful not to drive faster than is safe. You would not consider stabbing someone with a knife, but speeding can be just as murderous. Again, a girl shares her car date's responsibility. If she lets  the boy drive too fast, she shares the guilt if an accident occurs.

Courtesy on the Road

Courtesy on the road is important because it's the only safe way to drive. If you don't let the driver ahead of you get in line, you may cause a bad collision. If you refuse to give the right of way, you may not have another chance. Regardless of where you are, courtesy is expected and expedient. In a car, it is even more important.

HOW ABOUT BORROWING A CAR?

Sometimes, if the family car is not available, you may be tempted to try to borrow a car. You might consider asking your girl's parents to lend you their car. If they consent, because they trust you, then you come to a definite understanding with them as to what you will be responsible for. Naturally you will want to drive especially carefully and handle the car cautiously, as you would treat anything that belongs to someone else.

In most cases it's not a good idea to lend or to borrow

cars. If you have use of the family car, you would be taking a chance in lending it to someone else. Even if you know your friend to be a safe driver, it's better not to let him have your car. If someone ran into the auto, through no fault of your friend, you might still have a tough time explaining it to your folks. And you might lose your car privileges altogether.

Borrowing a friend's car can be just as bad. If there is an accident, whether or not you are to blame, you may find yourself in a tight spot. You could be the cause of your friend losing his car or his right to drive. If the car doesn't have proper insurance you may be in real trouble. Borrowing a car is just too risky.

CAR ETIQUETTE

When you accept the responsibility of driving a car on dates, you want to do what is expected of you. Helping a girl into and out of the car is the courteous thing to do. Especially if she's dressed up, she may need your help to prevent soiling her dress.

Honking Is for Geese

Parking before a girl's house and honking your horn is discourteous. The thing to do is to go to the door to meet your date. If her parents are home, you should go in and speak with them a moment before leaving. Let them know the details of the date, assure them that you will drive carefully, and tell them when you will be home. Your date's parents may still be uneasy about car dates. If you show some responsibility in calling for their daughter properly, they have more trust in you.

A girl can let her date know that she doesn't approve of

honking. She remains in the house until he calls for her in the accepted manner. Or she can go to the door and say, "Hi, Joe, come on in." Although a boy may be nervous about meeting a girl's parents for the first time, inwardly he is flattered by her action. Once he knows what she expects of him, he naturally goes to the door to get her.

DATE'S END

After a pleasant evening it's natural to want to sit a while in front of a girl's house and talk. Many parents, however, are concerned when they see the car parked out front too long. Also, neighbors may get the wrong impression when these sessions last more than a few minutes. If your parents are up and you want to talk some more, invite your date in for a Coke or cocoa.

It's up to the girl to ring down the curtain on a date. When they arrive at her home, she can signal that she's not interested in prolonged car conversations by opening the car door. At this point, the boy walks his date to the door, and unless he's invited in, makes his brief good night and leaves.

Parking and Petting

Parents and teen-agers alike are concerned about "parking." Many questions come up regarding whether or not to park, and how to prevent unfortunate incidents in a car. When you start to drive, the responsibility for "safe parking" as well as safe driving is both yours and your date's. For a detailed discussion of this problem, see page 190.

SUMMING UP

A boy should not feel out of things if he doesn't have a car for dates. When it comes down to cases, most girls would much rather go by bus than not go out at all. If a boy is fun to be with, his having a car is not too important to the girl.

An enterprising lad does not let the lack of a car keep him from asking a girl for a date. There are many things you can do without a car. If you live in a place with nearby public transportation, the problem is simple. Even if you live in a rural area without buses, streetcars, or trains, you are still not cut off from activities. You can usually get a lift from someone with a car, and for special events your parents probably would be glad to drive you.

You can always plan interesting dates at home, and you may even enjoy just going for a long walk. Some teen-agers bicycle into town for a movie just for the fun of it. Especially in good weather, you may want to plan dates which involve hiking or biking.

Having a car for dates is fun when the car is used correctly. But like a lot of money, it's not really necessary for a good time.

11

HOW TO SAY "NO"

Everyone has to say "No" at times. Sometimes it's easy, but most of the time it's hard. Adults have to say "No" when asked to do something that's against their principles. Very important is learning how to say "No" when you're invited to do something you'd rather not do. You will want to learn how to refuse an invitation without hurting the feelings of the person who asks you.

THE QUESTION OF LIQUOR

More and more the problem of drinking among young people comes up. Teen-agers and young adults throughout the country are faced with the question: "Should I take a drink?" Here are some things to consider as you make your decision.

Why People Drink

Many people, when asked why they drink, simply say, "Because I enjoy it." But drinking is usually more deeply motivated than that. There are many different reasons why people drink. The most common reason is to relieve feelings of insecurity. If everyone else is drinking, a person feels left out of things if he doesn't take a drink. People who call themselves "social drinkers" depend upon alcohol to keep them in good spirits and to keep the conversation rolling. They lean upon drink as a sort of social crutch. If they don't feel at home in a situation, alcohol loosens them up and makes them feel more congenial and sociable.

The danger is that as social drinkers depend more and more upon alcohol to provide their entertainment, the drinking can get out of hand. They begin to realize that they *must* have a cocktail before they can relax. Sometimes it even gets to the point where they feel physically ill unless they are continually stimulated by alcohol. They have let drinking become a necessity.

Alcoholics are usually people who feel neurotically insecure and unsure of themselves. They feel that they are inferior to others and unable to face the world. They use alcohol as an artificial stimulant to give them a temporary sense of security. They lose themselves more and more in the habit, forsaking everything else. If they are lucky, these people end up in the hands of competent workers who help them realize that they can exist without alcohol. Less fortunate alcoholics may literally drink themselves to death.

Teen-agers often start to drink because of social pressure. When others in a group are drinking, they feel that they also are expected to. They're afraid to refuse for fear of being considered "sissy." Some young teen-agers drink in an effort to appear more sophisticated than they are.

An occasional young person drinks as an act of rebellion against parents who forbid it, in an unfortunate effort to "show them" who's boss. While some independence is to be expected during the teen years, rebellion by way of unwholesome pursuits can be, and often is, harmful at the time—and for years ahead.

Are You Expected to Drink?

Young people rightly want to belong. There is a strong urge to conform and to do what the group expects, especially during the teen years. What many young people fail to recognize is that it is the person who does *not* drink who conforms to what is generally expected.

Continuing polls of young people conducted by Purdue University indicate that the overwhelming majority disapprove of drinking. The latest survey in 1957 found 60 per cent definitely opposed to drinking and another 12 per cent saying that although they were undecided they probably disapproved.

Whether or not you personally are expected to drink depends almost completely upon your family and your crowd. Some groups of young people include social drinking as a part of their activities. If their parents drink, young people are much more likely to be expected to drink. Other groups of young adults feel that drink is not necessary. They do not like to rely on artificial stimulation to keep their affairs interesting. They feel that they have resources enough in themselves not to have to depend upon alcohol. If you go with a crowd that drinks, they probably expect you to drink. However, if you wish, you can find other friends who choose not to spend their leisure hours and money on drink.

To Drink or Not to Drink?

If you're out with a group that is drinking you may feel that you are obligated to take a drink yourself. You may be afraid that the crowd will call you "chicken" if you refuse to drink. Social pressure is difficult to oppose. Many teen-agers, however, have found for themselves effective measures for refusing drinks without seeming prudish.

"I'll Have Coke"

If you want to keep peace among your friends, don't sound off on the evils of alcohol when you are offered a drink. It's not necessary to make others feel uneasy. When asked what he wants to drink, one boy brightly replies, "I'll have Coke, *straight,* please." This approach provides an easy out. His friends are amused at his remark rather than irritated by his refusal. He often finds others having their Coke straight too.

Maybe they just needed a way to say "No." If you know for sure that you *want* to refuse the drink, your problem in refusing is not difficult.

Principles Pay Off

If you're out with a person who wants to drink, and you yourself don't drink, what do you do? How can you let him know how you feel about drinking without making him think you are prudish? One teen-age girl reports that she was very concerned when her crowd started to drink. She didn't want to drink and preferred that her date abstain also. At first she was afraid to mention it, but later, when she finally did, she found that her date was actually relieved. He was not eager to drink, but he was afraid it was expected of him. Actually he had much more respect for her, as a girl of principles, than when he assumed she blindly followed the crowd.

Drinking and Driving

Drinking and driving are a bad combination. The papers often report accidents caused by people who felt they were sober enough to drive. Tests show that alcohol slows down your reaction time to an alarming extent. Even if you are feeling perfectly all right, you're an unsafe driver if you have been drinking. Many people realize this and leave their cars at home when they think they will be served liquor. If your escort has been drinking through an evening, and you have not, it's for your own safety to ask for the keys so that *you* can do the driving. If you can't drive, you'll probably want to make some other arrangements for getting home.

Drinking and Sex

As people drink they begin to lose their higher controls. The more they drink, the more uninhibited they become. Girls have gotten into serious trouble under the influence of alcohol. If a boy has had something to drink, it's harder to put off his sexual advances. He does things when he has been drinking that he would never consider doing when sober. Then both he and the girl must face their regrets the next morning—and all too often through the years ahead. Teen-agers generally find that drinking and sex are a dangerous combination.

THE QUESTION OF SMOKING

Smoking is accepted among some people as a natural thing to do. Others find that it's an annoying habit. Continuing research linking excessive smoking with lung cancer has caused many people to decide that smoking is just not worth the risk involved. Whether or not you smoke depends upon your background and personal feelings.

Why People Smoke

Smoking usually starts as a form of rebellion against authority. Teen-agers in the process of breaking the ties that bind them to their parents often use smoking as a form of rejection of their childhood. They feel that smoking makes them more "grown-up" in the eyes of their peers. Smoking may also be a manifestation of oral craving, arising out of insufficient sucking as a child. This oral craving is relieved by smoking or is sometimes satisfied by eating or chewing gum.

Smoking Is Habit Forming

One of the main problems of smoking is that it's habit forming. If you have successfully broken away from the strong ties you had with your family, you may no longer need smoking to assure yourself that you're grown-up. By this time, however, smoking has become such a habit that it's difficult to stop. It is true that many people attempt to stop, and some people actually do make the break, but, generally, people have great difficulty in stopping completely. One person wisely remarked that giving up cigarettes was easy—he had done it hundreds of times! Smokers usually admit that smoking is an expensive and messy habit. But some individuals feel that it provides enough relaxation to be worth the disadvantages. Others feel that it's not worth the trouble, and if they never start, they will never have to worry about stopping.

Think about It

If your crowd is one in which the majority of members do *not* smoke, you may have no difficulty deciding against it. But if your friends do smoke, you may have more trouble making up your mind. It's difficult to be different, especially when you are in your teens. As you come to realize that people do accept you as an individual, you won't have to "go along with the gang" in everything they do.

As an individual, you may recognize that it's important to do some careful thinking before making up your mind about smoking. Consider all the advantages and disadvantages. If you realize fully what you are getting into, and still feel that it's worth it, at least you will know what to expect. If, after weighing the evidence, you decide that it's simpler not to start smoking, your definite decision will help you when you have to refuse a cigarette.

"No, Thank You"

When people smoke, they feel it's courteous to offer others cigarettes. You do not have to accept if you don't want to. At the same time, you can refuse politely, without making any remarks about cigarette addiction. A simple "No, thank you" is sufficient. When people offer cigarettes to others it's

just a casual, almost mechanical, gesture, and a refusal is hardly noticed. If you feel that an explanation is needed, you can simply say that you don't smoke. Regardless of how strongly you feel about smoking, it's better not to condemn others.

THE PROBLEM OF NARCOTICS

Some teen-agers have parties specifically planned for smoking. Especially if their parents disapprove, they may feel the need for smoking secretly. It gives them a thrill to know they're doing something their parents disapprove of behind their backs.

This attitude is very immature, and such parties can be dangerous. The teen-agers who attend them are easy prey to dope peddlers who "contribute" marijuana. Young people may be tempted to try a "reefer." They have been promised an immediate emotional sensation. It may be very hard to refuse "just one" when everyone else is experimenting. Of course if the peddlers believed that it would remain at "just one," they wouldn't distribute "free" samples. They know that many of the people who say "just one" will continue taking "just one more."

Smoking marijuana is a first step toward dope addiction. Soon the marijuana is not enough, and young people are compelled by an insatiable craving to go on to heroin or other more potent drugs. Once you are "hooked" it is almost impossible to stop without long hospitalization and treatment.

Former policewoman Lois Lundell Higgins reports that juvenile addicts spend over $250,000 a day on narcotics. Addicts go to any extreme to obtain money for more dope. They steal and get involved with criminal gangs. Even morally sensitive people get into real trouble when they are under the influence. When in need of a "fix," nothing else matters; they will go to any lengths to get it. "Playing around" with dope is courting serious physical and emotional damage!

THE QUESTIONABLE SPOT

The time will come when you will probably be invited to a place that you're not sure you ought to visit. Perhaps your friends want to go to that roadhouse that has always looked dangerously intriguing. Maybe they want to go to a public dance hall of which your parents disapprove. What should you do?

The first thing to consider is *why* you are questioning this particular spot. If it's definitely the type of place you consider taboo, your problem is simple. But suppose you're not sure in your own mind about it. Maybe you have just heard rumors; maybe your parents have just dropped vague remarks against it. If you ask around, you will probably find out just why that place is considered off limits by some people. Knowing will help you decide what you want to do. Even if you know

something about the place, you may still be tempted to go—
just to see for yourself what it's like.

"Crazy Mixed-up Feelings?"

Very often teen-agers find that they have a conflict of
feelings. You may know that a roadhouse is not suitable for
you, but inwardly you very much want to go. Going to that
public dance hall may sound thrilling to you. You may be
curious to find out for yourself just what it's like. Yet you
know your parents wouldn't want you to go. Until you get
your own reactions straightened out, it will be hard to
explain to the others how you feel.

Pro and Con

If you have a question about places to which the crowd
might want to go, it helps to decide ahead of time if you would
feel comfortable there. One thing you might do is to find out
why your friends want to go there. Is it because they really
enjoy themselves or is it for a risky "thrill"? Do they really like
the spot, or do they go just because they are not supposed to?

Once you know these things, weigh the pros and cons.
How much fun do you think you'd have, knowing that you
shouldn't be there in the first place? How would you feel if
you were seen by some of your other friends or neighbors?
What if your parents found out? Most teen-agers feel that
it's wise to avoid doing anything which they would be ashamed
to talk about later.

Getting Off the Spot

Saying "No" is not so difficult once you have decided
against the place in question. If you really believe what you
say, it will be easier for you and more acceptable to your
friends. If you are hesitant and say something mealy-mouthed

like "Maybe I had better not go," the others may tease you. But if you are sure of yourself and firm in your reply, they will accept your answer.

One good way to say "No" is to offer an alternative suggestion. Follow up your refusal with an idea that may interest the others. When asked to go to a gambling joint, one boy answered, "I'd rather not go there; let's go down to the skating rink instead." Usually there are others in the group that would just as soon do something else.

The young people in one community complained that there was no *nice* place to which they could go on a date. The only places open after school games or movies were spots where liquor was served and where a rough gang hung out. When this fact was brought up at a young people's meeting one Sunday night, the leader and a committee of teen-agers were delegated to work with some of the city fathers toward the establishment of a YMCA in the town. Their proposal was publicized in the community, and soon it was widely discussed among responsible adults. Within a month one of the nicer ice cream stores offered to stay open late enough to be of service to the young people. A joint committee of young people and adults was then formed to consider permanent possibilities for a YMCA, with a trained youth worker and facilities for a wide variety of wholesome recreation. Is this something that you and your friends could do? Is there a vacant building, store, or hall which, with the help of interested adults, you could turn into a youth center?

PARTY OUT OF BOUNDS

Sometimes you're at a party that has gotten out of hand. Perhaps there is drinking that you had not anticipated. Maybe it has turned into a petting session. Some teen-agers are

12

FALLING IN AND OUT OF LOVE

not to condemn others when you have to refuse. Saying "No" in a courteous, tactful manner expresses subtly how you feel about the activity, without making the others think you dislike them as persons. The most effective way to do this is with humor. If asked to go gambling, you might say "Gambling?—I need my shirt!" Letting the others know you are not interested helps in avoiding unfortunate situations later. Doing it tactfully prevents hard feelings.

Perhaps the most important thing to consider when saying "No" is to offer alternative suggestions. If you follow up each "No" with a more attractive possibility, you may find it easier, both for yourself and others. One girl carries a package of mints in her purse. When offered a cigarette she says, "No thanks, would you like a mint?" In this manner without making an issue about the cigarette, she refuses politely and changes the subject.

Saying "No" need not be too much of a problem. When you yourself have definitely decided, you refuse the invitation in a tactful way and offer alternative suggestions that free you for more congenial activities.

time to act is the moment the party starts to get rough. It does no good to wait until the next morning and then condemn the host.

What Can You Do?

Try to get some activity started to pull the party back in line. Suggest one that would be fun—really fun—to absorb the guests. Perhaps a game of charades will liven things up. Maybe there are enough table games around to capture people's interest. How about a spur-of-the-moment scavenger hunt? Or maybe everyone would like to go out to the kitchen and make hamburgers or popcorn balls.

If a gang of boys try to crash a party, are you prepared to handle the situation? Do you know how to get help if they come looking for trouble? Many of the incidents that happen at parties can be avoided if each young adult takes responsibility for seeing that things run smoothly.

If you find that you can't help keep the party under control, the next best thing is to leave. If people are drinking too much and you're not enjoying yourself, simply explain to your hostess that you had better be running along. No one has much fun at a party that has gone out of bounds. After you have left such a party, reflect on it a while. Maybe you can prevent it from happening next time—especially at *your* party!

SUMMING UP

Saying "No" does not have to be difficult if you follow some simple principles. First, be sure in your own mind how you feel. If you're hesitant yourself, it's much harder to convince others. Try to make up your own mind firmly before you say anything. Second, be tactful in saying "No." Try disgusted, because parties so often turn into unpleasant situations.

Usually parties get out of bounds because of insufficient planning. If the activities and games are planned for a party, it is unlikely that it will degenerate. People find no need particularly to turn away from relaxing fun and entertainment to other veins.

Sometimes there are parties without adults on tap. Chaperons may seem old-fashioned, but it does help to have adults at social affairs; their very presence keeps things under control. Regardless of how carefully you plan parties, incidents may arise that need a firm adult  outlook. Suppose some fellows try to crash your party, bringing liquor with them. This is a hard situation for you to handle alone, but your parents would be able to put a stop to it at once.

Who Is to Blame?

When a party gets out of hand it's usually blamed on the hosts or hostesses. True, much of the fault is theirs. If they had planned the party properly, and made sure adults were present, the trouble might not have started. In one sense, however, every person at a party is responsible when it gets out of control. If you're at a gathering, and it seems to be getting wild, you might try to help steer it back to safety. The

Of course, you will fall in love. Falling in love is a part of dating. In fact, most young people fall in and out of love several times during their teen years. It's normal to grow fond of members of the other sex with whom you associate and share interests and have good times.

Learning to love and to be loved is an important part of growing up. But it can be confusing. When love feelings come so rapidly, so often, and with so many expressions, how is a girl or a boy to know how to behave? How do you handle these strong feelings? What happens when your heart is broken and love is lost? How do you recover from love's hurts? And, most important of all, how can you know when you are *really* in love—enough to make plans for the future?

NOT ONCE BUT MANY TIMES

Each of us loves many, many persons in many different ways during a lifetime. We start by loving our mothers and the other members of our families while we are still infants. We move on to love our playmates. And then we love anyone who is nice to us. As we get into the second decade of life, loves come and go in kaleidoscopic profusion as we find ourselves drawn to many other persons of our own and the opposite sex.

The evidence is that the average teen-age girl falls in love with about a half-dozen boys before she finds the man with whom she wants to spend the rest of her life. This is not to suggest that girls are emotional athletes, nor that either sex is to be considered fickle. It simply means that falling in and out of love is part of growing up.

Lusty Love

With adolescence comes the stirring of physical maturation that is deeply moving to members of both sexes. Hands brush in passing, and the blood pounds in one's ears. A desire to be close, to touch, to possess, to have and to hold one's lover, wells up recurrently with crescendos of feeling that are bafflingly urgent. A girl may be perplexed by her sexy thoughts and dreams. A fellow may be amazed that brief encounters with the opposite sex can cause such strong, intense, and urgent sex feelings. To the inexperienced young person, these surging sex-toned emotions which are so new, so powerful, and so insistent may be confused with "the real thing." Sexual attraction is one facet of love, but only one. There are other kinds of love that are just as much a part of relationship between the sexes.

Tender Love

Before long, the dating boy and girl may find that they are becoming fond of one another in a warm, gentle way. He is protective and considerate of her. She is thoughtful and kind to him. They discover a tender sympathy growing up between them that is sweet and meaningful. This, too, is a part of love—a very important part, both in dating and in life together through the years.

THE COURSE OF LOVE

It is generally recognized that the course of love rarely runs smoothly. But it took two university professors to plot the course that love takes in the lives of actual young people. Professors Kirkpatrick and Caplow found that the most usual course of love is one starting with mutual indifference and moving upward through attraction to love, and then either dropping again to indifference, with the broken love affair, or remaining in love at a high level of mutual involvement.

One out of every five love affairs studied is irregular in its course, with unpredictable shifts from love to hate to indifference to liking in various combinations throughout

the history of the relationship. Somewhat fewer young men and women experience an even more vacillating kind of love that is off-again-on-again, with ups and downs like a roller coaster's.

Experience teaches that while being in love is fine while it lasts, there are many love affairs that fail to grow into anything important. So the question arises: How can one recognize infatuation for the short-lived thing it often is?

IT MAY NOT LAST

There is a tendency to believe that one is in love as long as it lasts, and that any love that did not last must have been infatuation. The formula is a simple one: if it *was,* it was infatuation; if it *is,* it is love.

Not Really Blind

Love is blind, so the old adage goes. It is true that those who are deeply in love, as well as those who are madly infatuated, tend to idealize each other. They see only perfection in one another. They are blind to the human frailties, the foibles and follies, that are common to all men and women. But the love that lasts through the years has enough realism to protect the partners from being too grossly disillusioned about each other. They see one another and themselves clearly enough so that further acquaintance is a pleasant adventure rather than a painful discovery.

This may be the reason why lasting love is usually based upon full acquaintance. The two people grow more and more fond of each other as time goes on. They grow into love rather than just fall into it. They find each other lovable through actual experience and not just in fantasies. They have a love that is based upon reality, and it lasts precisely because it is real.

A Change for the Better

A young lover may protest that his love will never change. But if it is to last it will have to change and grow with time. As two persons develop and share new roles and tasks in life, their relationship with each other must shift to fit new situations. This doesn't mean that married people are any less in love than they were during their courtship days. There are few couples who could stand the strain of consuming passion day after day. But there are many who live out a full lifetime of quiet, loving devotion to each other in their common life together.

Two people at the altar quite probably love each other differently than they did when they first met, or than they will after the honeymoon is over, or the first baby has come, or the first family crisis is past, or when they share their later years together. If their love lasts, it must be as flexible as they are, to stretch up and out as they do to encompass more and more of life.

SUMMING UP

Dating is a proving ground for love. Loves arrive and are given a whirl on the dating merry-go-round that is common during the teen and young adult years. Most of these loves will last only a short while. Each new special friend, each new relationship, each new feeling, helps the person gain experience in the wonders of human interaction and insight into himself. As loves come and go, the emotional repertoire of the individual is developed to the point where he or she is increasingly capable of loving widely and deeply in the many ways that are important for fulfillment.

Loving and being loved is terribly important for the welfare of any person. It is necessary for a sense of well-being. Without it a person is lonely, cold, cut off from others. With love, there comes a feeling of relatedness with the whole world.

Learning to love and to be loved is not all pleasant or painless. Some experiences during the teen years are difficult, but none need be disastrous. There probably will be heartache in the lives of most young people—as there always has been. But fortunately, the heart does not break; it merely opens a bit wider for each new experience.

Falling in and out of love is to be expected as part of dating experience. It can be maturing as it is assimilated by any young person who wants to grow through it.

13

EXPRESSING AFFECTION

"Should I express affection on a date?"

"Must I kiss a boy good night?"

"How far should I go in necking?"

These are some of the questions boys and girls everywhere ask. There are many more, for young people want to know what is acceptable in this delicate area of a relationship. Problems centering around parking and petting are universal now, with so many dates taking place in automobiles. Public opinion is still a matter of concern to young people. Many questions are asked about why parents worry about dating behavior, and how other teen-agers feel about a public display of affection.

SHOULD HE OR SHOULDN'T HE?

Many a boy is puzzled about just what a girl expects of him when he takes her out. He brings her home from a date, and she either seems scared about what he will do next, or she hesitates and seems to be waiting for him to "try something." If he has not been out with her before, or if he has had little experience with girls, he just doesn't know what is expected of him.

That Good-Night Kiss

Teen-agers tend to agree that a first date is too soon for a good-night kiss. Some sophisticated fellows say, "Sure I try, but I don't really expect to get a good-night kiss the first date." If such a fellow does get the kiss, he may wonder

183

about how many other boys have also been so favored. This is exactly the impression a girl wants to avoid. No girl wants to appear "too easy." She feels it's better policy to give a boy something to come back for the next time.

Young people of both sexes tend to feel that a kiss should mean something besides just "good night." College and high school students usually agree that kissing should be postponed by a dating pair until they're fond enough of each other for the kiss to have special meaning.

Even though the first date is usually too soon for a good-night kiss, there are important exceptions. If a couple have known each other for a long time before they date, they may feel that a kiss is appropriate. If the two persons have had an especially good time together, a good-night kiss may be the only way in which they can express their satisfaction in being together. If the girl seems to want to be kissed, and the fellow is especially eager to do so, this too may be an exception to the general rule.

The Proper Moment

If the first date is generally too soon for a good-night kiss, how well should you know a girl before it is all right? is a question that boys often ask. This is a good question but difficult to answer, because the way two people feel about each other varies so greatly. With some girls a fellow will want to be amorous very soon, while with other girls intimacies don't seem necessary, or even desirable, even after long acquaintance. It's not just a matter of how long the two persons have gone together, but rather of what they have to express to each other which can only be communicated through kissing.

Signs and Signals

Boys are often puzzled about how to know just what expressions of affection a girl expects on a date. The girl's behavior is his best guide. If she leans toward him and looks at him expectantly, most boys assume that she wants to be kissed. Some fellows find that they can't rely entirely upon such signs of a girl's readiness, for when they try to kiss her she slaps or acts offended. On the other hand, a shy girl may not indicate her willingness, and yet want to be kissed. Asking a girl if he may kiss her seems to many a boy to be asking for a refusal. Sometimes a girl who would really like to be kissed is afraid the boy will think she's "fast" if she says "Yes." So, in general, it's best for a boy to wait until he knows a girl well enough so that he can interpret her reactions fairly accurately. That way his affectionate gestures will be welcomed rather than rebuffed.

How can a fellow know how far a girl will go in the expression of affection between them? If he respects her wishes, he "reads" her signals and obeys her signs of distress. When she draws back or requests him to stop by gesture or word, he breaks the chain of love-making and gets back on a comfortable basis again.

If he's a "love-pirate" exploiting girls with little regard for their feelings, he may get away with a few offenses, but sooner or later he will lose the confidence and friendship of nice girls. Sometimes a boy discovers that there are girls who make a game of love; they tease a boy only to laugh at him when he becomes affectionate. Such individuals, male or female, soon come to be recognized for what they are—and little love is lost on them.

No boy wants to be ridiculed for his love-making. Fellows

don't want to be rebuffed by girls they like. Most boys want to show affection to their girls in ways that will be mutually pleasant. Therefore the fellow does well to wait until he is fairly sure his girl shares his feelings before he proceeds with his wooing. Then he paces his expressions of affection to what seems appropriate and satisfying to both him and his date.

MUST YOU NECK TO BE POPULAR?

Necking is light love-making of the kissing, hugging, cuddling variety that stops short of becoming urgently sexually stimulating. Generally a girl who is fond of the boy she's dating enjoys his light caresses, especially if she feels that they're reserved for her alone. However, if a fellow has gained the reputation of being too ardent, then, quite likely, he will find himself being avoided by most of the nicer girls and dated only by those girls who "have nothing to lose" in dating a "fast" boy.

A fellow doesn't have to neck to be popular with the vast majority of girls. In fact, girls generally prefer boys who are interesting persons and popular among the fellows to those who are "ladies' men."

The same principle holds for girls—only more so! A girl doesn't have to neck or pet to be popular. In reality, surveys show that the most popular girls are rarely the ones who have a reputation for being willing to neck and pet on dates. It's the socially inept girl with few alternatives who most often is involved in necking sessions. The popular girl gets a reputation for being a pleasant companion, a good sport, and an interesting person. Necking is not a necessary part of her dating repertoire.

THE GIRL'S VIEWPOINT

There are all kinds of girls and women, just as there are all kinds of boys and men. Some girls are love-hungry in their search for affection and get the reputation of being "easy" and available. Other girls are too self-conscious, or too absorbed in other things, or too frigid to be at all interested in a boy's amorous advances. The majority of girls are neither afraid of familiarity, nor openly solicit it, but rather are puzzled about what boys expect and about how to keep their love-making within reasonable bounds.

Saying It without Kisses

Some girls have scruples against kissing too often or too soon or too promiscuously. They want to get to know and really like a boy before they let him become intimate. They don't want to get the reputation of being too free with their kisses.

Some health-conscious fellows and girls do not want to risk catching any of the diseases spread by mouth with indiscriminate kissing. Cold sores and other infections can run through a high school or college population, causing a great many sensible young people to realize the risks involved in promiscuous kisses.

How can you prove to a boy that you like him without yielding too soon to familiarities? That is an age-old question. Some boys just won't take "No" for an answer. Others act offended and hurt when they're held off. But the boy who likes a girl for herself will respect her wishes and not force himself upon her. So a girl has to run the risk of losing the attention of a few "wolves" in her search for the kind of date who is willing to be a genuine friend.

Letting a boy know what your standards are is one way of helping him accept them. You needn't do this in a preachy way. You might discuss other people's behavior or let your boy friend in on your dreams, aspirations, and values. A nice boy respects a girl with high standards and likes her all the more for knowing that she has not given other fellows the favors she refuses him.

Showing a boy you like him without expressing affection physically can be done in innumerable ways. You might express interest in what he is doing and planning; really listen to what he tells you; be sympathetic when he is in trouble; act pleased at his successes. Showing pleasure when you meet him, looking into his face when you speak to him, smiling warmly when he says something you appreciate, making him some simple little gift, inviting him to social affairs—all these are ways a girl tells a fellow she likes him.

When a Fellow Gets Fresh

When a boy goes beyond what pleases a girl in his love-making, she faces a difficult problem. If she allows him to continue, against her wishes, she may be headed for more trouble than she will be able to handle. If she tries to restrain him, she must know how to do it without hurting his feelings or making him feel rejected as a person. This calls for delicate know-how that a girl must learn—in action.

The inexperienced girl may wonder, "If he tries something, shall I slap him and run, or just run?" The more mature girl knows that she doesn't need to resort to either slapping or running in order to deal with the too amorous boy friend. She wards off unwelcome behavior with a firm refusal to co-operate, accompanied by a knowing smile and a suggestion of some alternative activity. She may say, "Not now, Ambrose—let's go get a hamburger; I'm hungry."

Or she may take a tip from Marianne. When her date seems about to do something objectionable, she takes both his hands in both of hers, squeezes them affectionately, grins into his eyes, and says, "You're quite a guy." By doing this, Marianne lets her date know that she won't go along with his intimacy, at the same time that she shows she likes him as a person.

A girl's best protection is in *anticipating* a situation and deflecting it. The wise girl who wants to avoid a necking session keeps up an animated conversation about things that interest her date until she is returned to her door, when she bids him a pleasant adieu and goes in. This is easier said than accomplished. But if the girl is sure of her objective, she avoids anything that points in another direction. She keeps to brightly lighted, well-populated places and away from dark lonely corners where the situation may get out of hand.

It is a wise girl who knows the variations on the "Come up

and see my etchings" theme well enough to decline an invitation to drive to a lonely Lovers' Lane "to see the view." This kind of know-how often comes from talks with other girls. As girls pool their experiences they can share their knowledge of various boys and their approaches. And they learn from each other the skills for dealing with various problem-boy situations.

PARKING AND PETTING PROBLEMS

In the good old days when most couples did their courting on the girl's front porch or in her back parlor, the question of parking and petting rarely came up. The girl's parents were usually close at hand, with one ear cocked for what was going on in the courting situation. One woman reports that her parents invariably appeared with a bowl of popcorn or a pitcher of lemonade at the precise moment when her lover became most amorous. Her parents explained that when the springs on the porch swing stopped squeaking, they would know it was time to "take something to the young people."

Nowadays when dating is often in automobiles, the young people are on their own from the time they leave the girl's front door. Where they go, and how far, and when they stop, and how long, and whether they keep their love-making within bounds is entirely up to the dating pair. This entails great responsibility requiring considerable know-how as well as know-why.

Sitting together in a parked car gives a dating pair privacy and quiet. In today's crowded homes, busy dormitories, and with the pressure toward group participation, parking may be the only way a boy and a girl can be alone together to talk. Couples who are genuinely interested in each other, perhaps planning for the future, certainly need such quiet times for developing a sense of unity. Differences come up that have to be ironed out in private. Dreams and ambitions must be shared. Plans must be laid ahead if the relationship is to grow and flourish.

No one objects to dating couples talking together in a parked car. It's the likelihood of petting that gives parking such a bad name. So many young people use the freedom of the parked automobile for unrestrained, irresponsible sexual activity that anyone who parks is suspect. In some communities police roam darkened areas where cars are parked, beam their flashlights into the cars, and send petting couples on their way. In one instance a man was arrested for kissing his wife in their own car! If petting is this much of a problem, it needs to be understood.

What Is Petting?

Petting is usually defined as anything a man does that is directly sexually stimulating to a female. In marriage, petting is the necessary foreplay that readies the woman to receive her husband. This behavior is complex and varied. It includes the deep and lingering kiss, the "French kiss," the fondling of the woman's body—especially those areas that generally are not exposed to view—and pressing all or part of the man's body close to that of his date or mate. The female may or may not participate actively in the fondling and kissing. She generally is relaxed and receptive, while the male is the more urgent and aggressive sexually.

Petting is distinguished from necking by its intensity and urgency. Young people themselves generally consider the lighter, gentler, tenderer types of love-making as necking. These are many and varied, taking in kissing, cuddling, holding the girl's head on the boy's shoulder with his arm around her waist, or cradling a boy's head in a girl's lap, sitting cheek to cheek, and as many et ceteras as there are variations on the old, old theme of love.

Young people find that there is a progression from the lighter to the heavier forms of expressing affection. It starts with a good-night kiss, goes on to necking, and may proceed to petting, heavy petting, and intercourse. In marriage this progression is uninterrupted. Among courting pairs most couples stop before the behavior gets too urgent, in conformity to what is expected of them as unmarried persons.

However, not all boys and men are responsible in their love-making. One coed reports that on her campus she is expected to give a good-night kiss on the first date, to neck on the second date, pet on the third, and that she has to fight for her honor the fourth time she's out with the fellow. This may not be typical. Yet enough problems occur in the park-and-pet situation to demand clarification.

Think before You Park

A girl need not feel obligated to park with a man she doesn't care for as a person. Letting a man exploit her as a female is no kindness to him, or to her. When an obviously exploitive male goes into his routine, any sensible girl will take heed and extricate herself as quickly and effectively as possible. In fact, if she's really smart, she will not be there on a car date with him in the first place. Unless she's sure that both of them have the same general expectations and plans, she won't accept a car date.

PARENTS HAVE A RIGHT TO WORRY

As soon as sons and daughters start going out, most parents worry that they will find dating situations too difficult to handle. Some of this concern comes from parents' own memories of their behavior as young people.

A recent cartoon portrays a mother seated in her bed, while Father paces up and down before the window. Through it we see the silhouetted heads of a couple seated close together in a parked car. (The girl is obviously daughter of the house.) Father is upset, worried about what the young people are doing. The mother is saying, "Come on back to bed, Father. Don't you remember when we were young?" And Father replies, "You're quite right, I DO remember—that's what I'm so worked up about."

A major concern of parents is that their sons and daughters don't get caught in some sexual jam that will spoil their future for years to come—perhaps catapulting them into a ruined reputation, or a loveless, unhappy marriage. Parents have invested a great deal in their children by the time the teen years come. They don't want to see their children hurt by situations and forces whose strength and urgency the young people may not be prepared to handle well. They want their children to grow up strong and well and happy. But few parents can discuss questions of love, sex, courtship, and marriage with their children to the point where they are sure that their children know all they need to know.

One recent study on a university campus reported that four out of five of all college freshmen said that they could not talk about love, sex, and courtship problems with their parents. Indeed, these were the most difficult questions of all to discuss at home in the experience of the majority of these college students. This reluctance of the younger generation to talk over with their parents the personal questions that bother them about dating is a cause for concern.

Young people who *can* and *do* discuss their problems with

adults whom they know and respect are fortunate. And their parents are fortunate, too, in being close enough to their own young people so that they know that they can be trusted.

Teachers Are People Too

Schoolteachers and principals are responsible for the conduct of students at school functions, within the school building, and in the neighborhood of the school. Let something happen that the public frowns upon, and it is the principal or the dean who must account for the episode. If couples are seen holding hands as they go from class to class, kissing in front of their lockers, or necking and petting at school par-

ties, some adults feel that something should be done to restrain these demonstrations. In order to protect the reputation of the school, some adult has to see to it that no one couple become obnoxious in their love-making.

Some teachers are more old-fashioned than others. They may have grown up in very formal, moral surroundings. They may be lonely, unhappy people who are peculiarly upset by emotional displays of any kind. They may be concerned that their students keep their minds on their school work and not get sidetracked by love and sex too soon. They may be deeply concerned about the future of certain students in whom they have special interest and faith.

In every school or college there are some adults who believe in young people and inspire their confidence. Such a teacher will "go to bat" for the students when some injustice has been done them by a particularly harsh disciplinarian. Even more important, this understanding teacher can help young people see what issues are involved and what social behavior is expected of them at school.

Reasonable young people do not label all teachers "old bags," but learn to respond to them as individuals, without being prejudiced against them simply because they're older people. Teen-agers don't like to be labeled "delinquents" or "hoodlums" just because some of their generation are. So, too, the younger generation needs to discriminate in their opinions about adults.

THE TEEN-AGERS' VIEWPOINT

In almost any community or campus there are some couples who are so open in their love-making that other young people feel responsible for correcting the situation. The annoyance of socially sensitive students at the behavior of some couples at dances and social affairs is understandable. They want their affairs to look "nice." They don't want to be embarrassed by conduct that is not suitable in a public place. They feel that it's unfair to those who don't date to carry on so obviously.

When young people themselves assume responsibility for their behavior at school and social functions, the adults in charge do not need to interfere. An overly demonstrative girl can be asked by the other girls to be more restrained. If this is done privately, perhaps in the powder room, neither the girl nor her date need be embarrassed. Similarly, a couple of fellows can pull aside an ardent male and suggest a less objectionable way of showing his affection.

DATES IN DORMS

Women's dormitories face the problem of keeping the conduct of dating pairs within respectable bounds. Girls who live in a college dormitory share the public lounges with several scores or even hundreds of other coeds for the entire college year. Any one girl cannot be as free with her visiting date as she could be in the privacy of her own home. She is expected to meet certain standards of conduct that are acceptable to her dormitory mates.

Just what constitutes socially acceptable dating behavior in a dormitory parlor has been the subject of discussion on many a campus. The girls themselves in dorm meetings tend to agree on the following standards:

> Keep the lights on.
> Do not close or lock the doors.
> Keep the feet on the floor.
> Show consideration for others.
> Acknowledge the dorm mother as the responsible adult at hand.
> Maintain a pleasant homelike atmosphere.

Such standards assume that dating pairs will enjoy the freedom of the situation by assuming responsibility for it. They acknowledge the rights of the nondating coeds as well as the privileges of the dating pair. They recognize the problem of the dormitory matron in maintaining decorum acceptable to the larger constituency. They grant that girls should be able to entertain their dates in an atmosphere that is pleasant and homelike within the dormitory parlors. They want dates to be welcome, responsible, and co-operative.

WHAT'S LACKING?

Necking and petting may become rampant where there are few other activities for dating pairs to enjoy together. In the town where there are active youth organizations, on the campus where there is a good social program, too much or too promiscuous love-making is not apt to be a major problem. This is a challenge to the community and the campus to provide a variety of wholesome functions in which both boys and girls can participate either as dates or as unaffiliated individuals. This is a responsibility for any or all of the persons involved. If such programs are lacking, young people should call it to the attention of their adult leaders and request that together some more adequate provisions be made for the social life of the community. Results do not appear overnight. But progress can be made if enough people care about the situation to work toward its improvement.

SUMMING UP

Love is one of the sweetest experiences known to humankind. In it a man and woman can express the highest and best that they know. It lies at the core of any courtship, and at the heart of the home. The expression of affection is nothing to be ashamed of or to feel guilty about. When two people love each other, each is a better person for the expression of their mutual feeling. Such significant sentiments are too sweet to spoil with shoddy makeshifts and promiscuous playing around.

The problem is not whether or not to express affection, but rather with whom, and when, and where, and how and for what purpose, and to what end. The answers to such questions must be discovered by each boy and girl. For in dates and dating, a boy and girl play out the eternal drama of the sexes in whatever roles they believe theirs to be—with each other, and in life.

14

SEXUAL RELATIONS BEFORE MARRIAGE

You may not be dating long before you meet up with the question: Why not go all the way? Premarital chastity used to be taken for granted. Today some people question it as a standard of behavior. Others openly brag of their own premarital experience and urge the uninitiated to do likewise. Now more than ever it is necessary for a young person to decide upon personal standards of sexual conduct.

GOING ALL THE WAY

Our society allows a great deal of freedom to young people. It says, in effect, to dating pairs, "Go on out and have yourselves a good time. Enjoy each other in a variety of situations. You have privacy, an automobile, and no chaperonage. Get acquainted with each other. Become fond of one another, and make plans for the future, if you wish. But one thing is to be left for marriage—going all the way."

Research studies indicate that the majority of young persons feel strongly that premarital chastity is important. Investigations on large coeducational campuses both before and after World War II indicated that *two-thirds* of both men and women students believed in *no* sexual relations for either sex before marriage.

The famous Kinsey reports are often misquoted to suggest that immorality is rampant among the younger generation. The fact is that more than half of the college men and women reported that they had no sexual relations before marriage. And, of the women who did, more than half had their experience only with the men they married. Concern for morality was given by nine out of ten of the women as the reason why they restrained from going all the way.

Many people recognize that the standards of society require premarital chastity. As Americans we pride ourselves on sportsmanship and playing according to the rules. Most of us agree that it's not funny to cheat. We don't apologize for straight dealing in sports or in business—why should we in our personal relations?

Who Goes All the Way?

The tendency is to divide people into two groups: those who have not, and those who have had premarital experience. Actually there are great differences among those who have had sexual relations before marriage. There is the boy or girl who once stepped over the line and ever since has refrained. There is the girl who has known many men intimately, and the one who gives herself fully only to the man she is about to marry. There are others who indulge promiscuously whenever and with whomever they can. There are those who are demanding, exploitive, and sexually aggressive, while others are tender, considerate, and mutual in their love-making. There are those whose mating is chiefly biological, and others who express in sexual union deep spiritual and emotional communication.

Clinical and statistical studies to date indicate at least five kinds of people who go all the way before marriage, as distinguished from those who do not:

First is the unconventional person with few or no religious roots. More devout young people tend to be faithful to the mores—and to one person, in marriage.

Second is the young person from the lower socioeconomic group. (Not all, of course—but those who were brought up without high moral standards.) In general, the middle-class boy or girl values chastity more highly, and more often refrains from going all the way before marriage. That is probably because the young person who has high aspirations for his future has more at stake and more worth waiting for than does the less privileged youngster.

Third is the person who has a need for love—at all costs. These are the emotionally hungry persons who will do any-

own rules. Those who conform don't need to explain why. Those who break with custom must defend their position. This is one reason why the arguments for premarital sexual relations are heard so often and so loudly.

In Serious Trouble

A major concern for any girl contemplating premarital relations is that she might "get into trouble." In spite of recent advances in population control, there is no completely sure protection against pregnancy. Even among married couples using accepted methods of birth control, many unplanned pregnancies occur. The problem is greater and has much more serious consequences for unmarried persons.

The unmarried mother faces a terrifying set of problems. Where can she go? What will she do with her baby? How will she protect her educational and vocational plans? How can she safeguard her reputation? Will the father of her child marry her? She fears the wrath of her parents, and oftentimes feels guilty that she has brought disgrace upon her family.

Even if the girl doesn't become pregnant, her feelings of guilt and shame about premarital sex and her fear of detection may be intense. In her effort to right things after sexual relations have been established, she may beg her sweetheart to marry her, only to find that her urgency for marriage displeases him. Premarital affairs are known to break up because the girl's insistence upon marriage is in opposition to the fellow's reluctance to be pushed into it.

Girls usually feel that their chances for a future marriage are handicapped by having had premarital experience. They know how prevalent is the male "double standard." He is willing to "play around" with any girl who will allow it, but he seeks out a girl he feels he can trust to be the mother of his children—a girl who has maintained her standards of chastity before marriage.

Since time immemorial the woman has been called on to be the one who maintains sexual standards in a relationship. So the burden of the situation rests primarily on her. If she allows premarital intercourse, it is she who is generally considered the fool. If a pregnancy ensues, it is the girl who is "in trouble." Yet the fellow also has a stake in the situation.

His Future at Stake

One of the most difficult questions to answer is one that crops up in high schools, colleges, and youth groups, when a boy asks, "My girl is pregnant. Do I have to marry her?" He may feel that if he does not, he's a cad. But if he does, he may be forfeiting all his plans for the future—his education, his vocational dreams, his place in his social set. Even the secure position he holds within his family and circle of friends may be at stake in an unfortunate, premature marriage. He may realize that he does not really love the girl. He may wonder if perhaps she has trapped him into this predicament. He may be haunted by the question, "If she went all the way with me, how can I be sure there have not been others?"

Few fellows want to get stuck with "a tramp." The danger of venereal infection is real with a girl who tends to be promiscuous. And in spite of medical advances, venereal diseases are still widespread, especially among teen-agers. Even more important is a boy's distaste for being tied to a woman he cannot respect. Yet if a girl allows him to go all the way, she frequently does lose his respect.

Such sobering questions discussed among young fellows bring many of them to the realization that maintaining standards of premarital chastity is a responsibility for the man as well as for the girl. Indeed, as men get to talking about it, they realize that in some ways they are in a better position to know what is happening in a sexually toned situation than an inexperienced girl is. The fellow usually is aware of sexual stimulation earlier than the female is. Therefore if he realizes that his welfare, as well as the girl's, is involved, the outcome won't rest entirely with her—he will assume some responsibility for restraint himself.

If a fellow really loves his girl, he feels protective and tender toward her. He wants to safeguard what is beautiful and sacred in his love. During the Korean War, one young man in service overseas wrote about these feelings in a letter to his sweetheart:

> Three of us fellows here are engaged, and two are just dating heavily. The other night we got into a discussion of premarital intercourse that was very enlightening. You see, one of the engaged fellows had had intercourse with an ex-girl friend to whom he was once engaged. We found that he was rather sorry about the experience. He believed that intercourse was the direct cause of his breaking up with the girl. It seemed impossible to back out after it happened and so it was either "get married" or "break off." I sincerely think that our policy of no heavy petting and no lengthy French kissing will help us prevent any experience for which we might be sorry, especially in view of our long engagement.
>
> You know, darling, we will have to be very careful when I get back next September, so that we may protect that which we would like to keep pure until we get married. It's my love and respect for you that makes me want to have our marriage just right.
>
> Always remaining all yours, _____

WITHIN LIMITS

The boy and girl who want to maintain standards of pre-marital chastity are faced with the problem of keeping their relationship within bounds. This may be especially difficult if they are very much in love. When a girl loves her man, she wants to do anything that will bring him pleasure. So unless she has her own standards in mind, she may find it difficult to restrain him and herself from the full expression of their love for each other. This is even more of a conflict for the boy who loves his sweetheart so much that he can't endure not having her completely, yet at the same time knows that he must control his feelings.

Standards from the Start

Long before the one great love appears, both boys and girls usually have other preliminary little love affairs with

members of the other sex. If the individual has established a precedent for not overstepping the bounds in these previous relationships, it's probably easier when the "true love" comes along.

This doesn't mean that you have to remain aloof and coolly unavailable throughout your teen-years. Quite the contrary. The person who maintains high standards of personal conduct is often a popular, socially active individual with many interests, activities, and friendships. He enjoys the companionship of both sexes in a variety of situations. He learns in action the many pleasures to be found in socializing.

The maturing individual learns to give and to receive affection in a wide repertoire that offers expression to the many sides of love. He learns how to be tender, protective, comradely, romantic, dependent, nurturing, as well as passionate and erotic. Thus, by the time two people are ready to marry, they know how to love and to be loved in the many ways that it takes to make a union happy.

At the same time, the person who wants to maintain standards of premarital chastity must guard against those individuals and situations that make it difficult.

Choose Your Partner

A person who wants to keep within bounds in premarital sex behavior must be careful in the choice of dating partners. Some girls are exploitive and demanding in their relationships with men. Some young people date with intercourse as an objective for the evening. To be safe, a girl must be pretty sure of the fellow she is dating.

A recent study of male sexual aggression on a university campus reports that more than half of the coeds were offended by their dates' behavior at least once during the school year. The offensive behavior on the part of the males included necking, petting, and attempted intercourse, sometimes with violence. The largest percentages of offensive situations occurred on first or occasional dates (48.5 per cent) in contrast to 8.2 per cent among pinned or engaged couples. This indicates that the male "on the prowl" doesn't force himself upon a girl because he likes her. Quite the contrary, when he loves her he respects her and doesn't offend her with aggressive sexual behavior.

Girls who have found a boy hard to handle on a date frequently warn other girls to steer clear of him. This seems to be girls' chief protection from unscrupulous males. The girl who accepts a date with a man whose reputation she knows to be "fast" may be deliberately letting herself in for trouble.

Likewise, the boy who dates a girl labeled "easy" by other fellows may find himself sexually stimulated and tempted to the point where it's hard to control the situation.

It may seem smart or exciting to date a person with a reputation for being sexually demanding or available. But what starts as exhilarating may end up being depressing and degrading, as many young people have learned to their sorrow.

Why Take Risks?

The young person who wants to maintain standards of premarital chastity avoids dating the chance acquaintance, the pickup, the proffered ride in an automobile with a stranger, and all other potentially risky situations. Unscrupulous persons of both sexes are hard to distinguish from responsible, respectable ones at first meeting. Therefore the only real protection you have is in steering clear of situations that may become dangerous.

Staying out of compromising positions includes turning down invitations to obviously unsavory roadhouses, to motels, hotel rooms, or even to the home of your date if no responsible adults are to be present. Young people sometimes

Andy is a case in point. When he was a sophomore in high school, his girl became pregnant, dropped out of school, and left the community. He was allowed to stay in school but he was forbidden all extracurricular privileges. He had to leave the ball team. He was not allowed to attend school dances. He

was avoided by many of the fellows and most of the girls. He talked his unpleasant position over with his principal and his religious adviser, and they suggested that if he applied himself wholeheartedly to his work, his situation might improve in time. During his junior year, by dint of hard work and extra hours in the library, he made the best grades he'd ever had. He stayed out of mischief, got over his rebellious attitude toward his teachers, and began treating them with respect. He slowly regained the acceptance of both the adults and young people in his school. He never was elected the most popular boy in his class, but when he graduated he felt that he belonged. Most of the people who knew him looked upon the early unfortunate incident as something that was over and done with. It was a long hard pull, but Andy made it. He feels it was worth the effort now to be able to walk down Main Street and feel he belongs and is accepted.

SUMMING UP

The physical aspect of the attraction between boys and girls and men and women is very real, very powerful, and very important. It is made up of the creative energy that produces new human life. As such, it is not to be played with lightly or used for the thrill of a moment. Rather it is to be accepted with respect, appreciation, and a willingness to keep it in correct focus in one's own life.

The boy and girl who learn to enjoy each other in a variety of activities learn to share much more than just the fact of their maleness and femaleness. They build a friendship and share intellectually, emotionally, spiritually, as well as sexually. If they let the erotic part of their relationship crowd out the other elements in their friendship they find themselves cut off from other activities and other friends, and soon are so involved with each other that firm steps have to be taken—often to end the relationship.

Even in marriage there is much more to the husband-wife relationship than just being sexual partners. Marriage is more than a bed for the night; it is a home for the years. A husband and wife must learn to share their interests, their hopes, and their values if they are to make their marriage truly happy and lasting. Similarly, if a dating pair keep their relationship in focus, without letting any one aspect crowd out the others, they build a many-faceted friendship that is deeply satisfying.

The belittling of premarital chastity and marital fidelity by certain groups of people need not sway the self-respecting young person from his standards. Within faithfulness a person can be true to his love and to himself, enjoying the sweet peace of emotional security that comes from doing what is right for him.

15

GOING STEADY

When a boy and girl date only each other to the exclusion of anyone else, they are said to be "going steady." This is something new in dating practice. In former generations a courting pair might be "keeping steady company," but this usually meant that they were serious enough about each other to be planning marriage. Going steady nowadays frequently implies no such commitment to the future. It may come very early in a relationship. It may involve "an understanding" before getting pinned or engaged, or it may simply be a matter of mutual convenience with no plans or prospects for the future.

Going steady is a controversial question about which both young people and adults feel strongly. Some openly and vigorously oppose it. Others champion it quite as strongly. Many young people are genuinely confused about it.

214

Teen-agers have many questions about why adults tend to oppose going steady, about when to start going steady, about how to keep from going steady, and about how to get back in circulation again after breaking off with a steady. These are all important questions. The answers are not simple but they are discussable.

HOW ADULTS SEE IT

Some parents prefer their sons and daughters to go steady rather than to play the field. These parents state that they feel much safer when a son or daughter dates someone they know and like instead of a series of comparative strangers.

Far more numerous and vocal are the parents and adult leaders who oppose going steady. A particularly vigorous attack on the practice was made recently by the Director of the Family Life Bureau of the National Catholic Welfare Conference who was quoted in the press as saying:

> Going steady is pagan unless there is a reasonable chance of getting married within two years. The teen-age custom will have to be stopped if the concept of Christian marriage is to be saved.

This position reflects the concern of many adults. They feel that when a boy and girl see so much of each other, they are apt to become involved emotionally or sexually to the point where their futures are jeopardized.

WHY GO STEADY?

When the University of Michigan interviewed 2,000 girls between eleven and eighteen years of age in a nationwide study in 1956, approximately one-fifth of the girls were found to be in favor of going steady. The investigation revealed that older girls tended to approve of going steady more than younger girls did. Comparable data are not available for teen-age boys. But the pros and cons of going steady are so widely discussed by members of both sexes that it's possible to summarize the reasons young people generally give for going steady.

Safer and Easier

Boys generally agree that it's "just easier" to go steady than to date around. Teen-age boys say that when they date a girl regularly they know what she expects. They're more comfortable with a steady date than with a strange girl every time. They don't have to get up courage each time to ask a new girl for a date or run the risk of her refusing.

College boys frankly report that going steady is cheaper than taking a new girl out all the time. "The girl you haven't dated before expects you to show her the town," they say. "Your steady knows how you're fixed financially and so doesn't expect as much or as expensive entertainment."

Teen-age girls seem to feel that they're *safer* dating steadily than when they date around among many boys. They put it this way. "When you date good old Joe, you know what the evening holds and you're sure you can handle any situation that might come up while you're with him. With a strange boy, you can never be sure of what will happen, what he will expect of you, or whether you can manage the situations that may arise with him."

This may be the chief reason why going steady has increased in recent years. Now when so many teen-agers go to large consolidated schools or live in areas with transient or diversified populations, an individual can rarely be sure of what standards a date may have. In contrast, during "the good old days," dates were selected from a small, homogeneous neighborhood where everyone pretty much agreed on codes of conduct, and where the date was usually known not only by the girl but by her family as well. Then, too, dates were more carefully supervised by responsible adults; today's automobile dating makes such chaperoning impossible. Therefore young people today find that it's easier and safer to steady-date someone they know and trust than it is to risk a variety of expectations from the wide assortment of accessible young people.

Dating Security

Girls, especially, comment upon the social security they find in going steady. When a girl is not going steady she may not be able to get a date for the social affairs she wants to attend. She worries for weeks before the big events for fear that she will not be asked. Even a Saturday night date is dubious if she's not dating steadily. Going steady remedies all that—she's more likely to get to the big social affairs, and Saturday night dates are more assured.

A recent study shows clearly that girls who go steady have more dates than those who don't go steady. One simple reason is that the mutual expectation of going out together makes it easy for a boy to ask his steady girl friend for a date. It also makes it easy for her to accept, as a matter of course. Boys too report that having a date when they want one without having to scour available possibilities and face the chance of a "No" gives them a nice feeling of security.

Social Pressure

In some communities and on some campuses the practice of going steady is so well established that it's generally expected of everyone. Social pressure for going steady in such situations means that if you go at all, you go steady.

Here is a fairly typical picture. Joe takes Mary to a social affair on Friday evening; they are seen together on Saturday afternoon. By Monday they are considered to be going steady. Whether Mary and Joe have discussed it or not, the other boys assume that Mary is Joe's girl and so they don't ask her for dates. Simultaneously the other girls come to the same conclusion and assume that "Joe will do right by her." Before the two persons have had a chance to decide whether they want to go steady or not, they feel the social pressure so strongly that it's hard to resist. As a coed phrases it, "Have one or two dates with the same guy and you're stuck." Some fellows say that the fear of being "tagged" as belonging to a girl keeps them from dating at all, in many cases.

In the community or on the campus where social pressure toward going steady prevails, young people of both sexes need to learn (1) how to keep from going steady if they don't want to, and (2) how to stop going steady when they no longer find it promising. Both of these problems are considered later in the chapter. Now let us continue with further reasons young people have for going steady.

Preferring Each Other

There is such a thing as "prestige" dating. It occurs frequently in colleges or schools where a person is actually rated by the kind of date he has. When a high-ranking coed must date a BMOC (Big Man on Campus) in order to maintain her standing and please her sorority sisters, going steady is her way of maintaining her standing. Similarly, the BMOC whose name is linked with that of a high-ranking coed goes steady with her as a way of maintaining his social position

on campus. This process starts in high school where the most popular girl goes steady with the president of the senior class or the captain of the football team, not just because they like each other, but because they prefer to be seen together rather than in the company of a lesser catch.

Of course, sometimes two people genuinely prefer each other's company over anyone else available. When a couple are in love, whether it lasts permanently or not, they want to date only each other. Feelings of jealousy that so often accompany the early loves of teen-agers also tend to make one or both members of the pair resist dating anyone else.

There are couples whose affection and mutual preference for each other is mature enough to be the basis for future plans. Then, going steady leads on to further commitment.

Having an Understanding

Going steady is ultimately preliminary to getting engaged. The two people have an understanding that if they continue to care for each other they will, when the time is right, announce their engagement to marry. Having an understanding is a tacit recognition between the dating pair that they plan eventually to marry. It's similar to what their grandparents called "keeping steady company"—the step just preceding the posting of banns and the announcing of the engagement. Few persons have any objection to this kind of going steady. When two people are genuinely in love and "right for each other," they understandably want to date each other exclusively.

But what about the other reasons given for going steady— are some of them spurious? Aren't there times when going steady is *not* wise? What do young people themselves consider the disadvantages of going steady?

WHEN NOT TO GO STEADY?

Both boys and girls tend to feel that it's not wise to go steady just because you're pushed into it. When the social pressure in your community or school is so strong that you're tagged with anyone you have dated twice, then something must be done to offset such coercion.

The obvious solution is not to date the same person more than once or twice in succession. The girl who doesn't want to go steady will have to refuse a boy whom she has just recently dated, until she has been seen with others. A boy will take a given girl out only occasionally, be seen with a number of girls, and even go out occasionally with the fellows to show that he's not going steady.

Another way to avoid getting stuck is simply to let all your friends clearly understand that you do not consider yourselves "steadies," that you don't want your names linked together.

When It Limits Your Friendships

Let's face it, when you go steady you have less opportunity for getting to know other persons of the opposite sex. This means you as a girl are limiting your knowledge of the kinds of boys you should know before you can make a wise choice of a life partner. Conversely, the boy who goes steady with one girl doesn't get acquainted with enough other girls in a dating situation to know whether he really prefers his steady to other girls or not.

This is an especial concern of very young teen-agers who need to experience different kinds of dating partners in different kinds of dating situations. After a teen-ager has dated around for some time, he may want to focus on one preferred date, but in the early stages of dating there are many reasons why going steady is not wise.

When It Restricts Your Development

It is well known that human personality grows in relationship with others. Each of us is different with different people. Each close friend we have draws out a different set of responses from us and has a different kind of influence upon us. During the second decade of life most boys and girls are learning how they feel about members of the other sex. Especially in the teens, there should be enough friendships with different members of the other sex to enable you to know your emotional capacities.

Take young Sam as a good illustration. He found that he was in love with three different girls at the same time! The first was Ann who lived next door, and with whom he could discuss anything. Ann was a pleasant companion, a good sport. She really understood him, and he loved her for it. But he had never kissed her; in fact, he never even felt like it. His love for Ann was that of a comrade, a pal, a true friend.

But Rosie was the sort of girl who brought out all the male in Sam. He couldn't discuss much of anything with Rosie. But he didn't have to, for when he was with her, talking didn't seem important. His love for her was passionate, lusty, frighteningly intense.

Mary brought out still a different set of feelings. Mary went to his church, and when the two of them stood holding a hymnal together, the most uplifting feelings coursed through him. With Mary he thought big thoughts, he dreamed big dreams. He wanted to go out into the world and do things that would be worthy of the love he felt for her. In short, his love for Mary was spiritual and inspirational—the type that a man needs to find in a woman.

In truth, what young Sam was discovering was three different aspects of his own ability to love a woman. Each of the girls in his life was helping him develop three parts of himself that will be important in his future life as a man, a husband, and a father. No *one* of these three girls could promote a total development of personality for Sam. And no *one* of them would satisfy him for going steady too long. But someday, having developed a many-faceted capacity for love, he will find a woman who elicits in him his full ability to love and to be loved in these three ways, and more.

The person who starts going steady too soon may miss important aspects of his personality development that might be discovered through a variety of friendships. After experience with many persons has matured you, you can bring to a mature love relationship the rich repertoire of response that would have been impossible earlier.

When It Gets Involved

Two people who go steady see so much of each other that they are apt to get involved before they're ready to marry and settle down. They are likely to become emotionally or sexually entangled before they have developed the other facets of their relationship which will enable them to live together compatibly.

Sexual attraction between two people is a powerful urge that builds up to impressive proportions, especially if the two persons are in constant association. They begin to dream of each other even when they're apart. When they're close, they find their responses becoming more and more ardent, and more difficult to restrain.

One of the most frequent reasons that couples quit going steady is that their relationship becomes so emotionally explosive that they are practically blown apart. They either go further than they find comfortable in their love-making, or their frequent association builds up tensions that induce squabbles that eventually neither can stand. This is why if you care for another person, it's wise not to get into too tight and steady a relationship too soon or you will find yourselves heading for a breakup.

When Someone Gets Hurt

Going steady can result in heartbreak when one is more in love than the other. That member of the pair who takes the relationship more seriously is bound to be hurt when the break comes.

Sometimes it's the girl who tires of her steady first. Then she asks, "How can I get rid of good old Joe? He hangs

around all the time. He takes me for granted. Yet he hasn't done anything that I can pick a fight about. I just don't want to go steady with him any more."

One of the most frequent questions that college boys ask is how to get a girl back into circulation after going steady with her. The sensitive, thoughtful boy doesn't want to hurt a girl who counts on him. He realizes that she may have a hard time recovering from their affair. Yet he finds that he's desperately eager to be rid of her before she maneuvers him even more deeply into their unpromising relationship.

Sometimes two people mutually realize that the time has come for them to break off going steady. Even then the question arises as to how it can be done most effectively and comfortably for them both.

BREAKING OFF THE AFFAIR

Nowadays so many young people go steady with several persons before entering a relationship that leads to marriage that it becomes important for both sexes to learn how to break off with a steady when the time comes. Since terminating a relationship that has been meaningful is apt to be painful, the considerate boy or girl wants to know how to break things off without hurting the other person. "After all, she has invested the best months of her life in me, and I don't want to hurt her now," says a college boy.

Avoiding Each Other

There are some men who simply break off a relationship abruptly and finally by not seeing a girl again. Such a fellow makes his actions talk for him. He stays away. He does not call the girl. He avoids the places they used to frequent together. He sometimes goes out of town without leaving her a forwarding address. Or he is seen about town with another girl or with a group of fellows. By this time the girl realizes that they are not going steady any more.

A girl may not be quite as successful in this approach, because her boy friend is accustomed to coming to her residence, where she finds it difficult to avoid him. Even if she could, she might not want to break off this abruptly. A girl is more apt to taper off gradually in breaking up with a steady.

Young people who are sensitive of others' feelings realize that breaking off abruptly is unnecessarily harsh and hurtful. A thoughtful boy would rather part on good terms with his former girl friend than drop her suddenly. A girl would rather hear directly from a fellow that things are over between them than learn it from gossipmongers. She's humiliated if others are aware before she is that she's no longer going steady. And she's miserable during that period of uncertainty when she is no longer sure of her status.

Discussing the Break

Unfortunately, many a girl can't keep from going into long agonizing discussions of "how washed up we are." She may torment the boy with embarrassing questions such as, "What did I do to lose your love?" She may beg him to reconsider and take her back again. Such fanning of dead ashes rarely makes a relationship burst into flame again. On the contrary, it usually makes the break even more necessary for the boy and more difficult for the girl.

Some couples find that they can discuss their relationship without rancor, and decide in a friendly fashion that it's time to break up. They try to understand what led up to their break so that the experience can give them insight. Sometimes such a couple end up as friends.

Easing Off

An increasing number of young people seem to have such good rapport with each other that they can sense when their friendship should shift to another basis. These are usually mature individuals who have learned that friendships change as one develops, and that not all relationships last indefinitely. A boy and girl can recognize that although their friendship has been something special, with changed feelings and interests it has become pointless. Then it is that they can break off mutually without hurting one another.

These are the young people who often can help each other get back into circulation again after the breakup. Returning to the social whirl is a difficult step for many boys and for most girls, regardless of whether the end of the affair was painful or easy.

BACK IN CIRCULATION AGAIN

After a couple break off, there is something of an interval before either of them becomes re-established as a member of the dating crowd again. If they themselves can accept their breaking up fairly well, they can help each other get back into circulation once more in a number of ways.

Mary can let her friends know that she's at the point of breaking off with Tom. Then, as certain of her girl friends express an interest in him, she, more easily than anyone else, can arrange a date between them. Similarly, Tom could arrange a double date with Jack who's long had a yen for Mary. In the course of the date Tom can see to it that Jack and Mary get acquainted. If Tom and Mary still like each other, they can be of great mutual support during the trying period of transition until each of them begins to date again.

If the break has been painful, full of recriminations and regrets, then a couple may have to face the double problem of getting over their emotional scars and re-establishing themselves as best they can without each other's help.

Both of them may need a period of relative solitude in which to get back on their feet emotionally. They will devote more time to work, to friendships with members of their own sex, to activities with their families, until interest in dating again develops. Then they will let others know they are ready to accept invitations again that may lead to dating. Sometimes, going to another community for a while, visiting a relative, taking a trip or a vacation, helps a person get over a broken love affair and find himself or herself again.

GOING STEADY WHEN SEPARATED

Frequently the question comes up as to whether it is wise for a couple to try to go steady when they will have to be separated. She may have to go off to college; they may be heading to different campuses; he leaves for military service or a job in another community. What should they do then? Try to continue going steady during the period of separation? Or should they break off and make themselves available for a normal social life, since they're so far apart that dating isn't possible?

The answer seems to depend upon how much their relationship means to them. If they're devoted to each other, and feel that their relationship is definitely headed toward engagement and marriage, then very possibly they will attempt to maintain close contact through correspondence and visits and not date others during the period of their separation.

But if they have been going steady as a matter of mutual convenience, then their separation offers a pleasant way of moving on to other relationships. If neither of them is ready for permanent commitments as yet, they may agree that theirs has been a meaningful companionship, but now that they must part, they will date others and see what happens. If, when they're both ready to settle down, they still prefer each other to anyone else they have known in the interim, then they might well re-establish their relationship. In the meantime their freedom to date others has meant that they have kept alive socially and so are presumably more mature and ready for ultimate marriage than if they had been living in lonely isolation throughout the period of separation.

Deciding together whether it will be wise to date others during the separation is a constructive way of approaching the problem. If a couple mutually agree that dating others is wise, their problem is solved. If they both feel that they want to be faithful to each other, they then must figure out how to continue contact with each other, and with other persons generally, while they're so far apart. If the two disagree on policy in the matter of trying to go steady during the separation, time and continued efforts to find an acceptable solution to their dilemma will tell.

SUMMING UP

Going steady offers two young people a chance to get to know one another as personalities. As they date each other in numerous situations, they see each other as they really are. A girl who has gone steady with a boy over a period of time becomes able to anticipate his interests, to recognize his moods, and to meet his needs. As he gets increasingly well acquainted with her he becomes familiar with her reactions, wishes, standards, and values. In many ways going steady is good preparation for marriage in that it provides a couple with opportunities for becoming closely sensitive to each other as two whole persons. Through experience they have learned how to meet each other's need for companionship. As one fellow puts it:

"Going steady has done a great deal of good for both of us. We have learned to make sacrifices for each other and are making plans for the future. We have different opinions on things and we always talk them out."

When a couple start going steady before they're ready to settle down or assume responsibility for keeping their relationship on an even keel, they may be headed for painful situations and emotional distress. Real problems can result from rushing into exclusive dating without being sure of one's own readiness for the step. This is why steady dating among young teen-agers is so often questioned by the same people who approve of it for older, more mature young people.

Those who oppose going steady have a point. Those who feel that going steady has advantages are right too. Whether going steady will be wise or not for a particular couple at a particular point in their relationship, only they can tell. As they understand more about what is involved, they will be better able to make such a choice wisely and well.

6

GETTING MARRIED

Eventually dating leads to marriage. As two persons date each other more and more, they come to have feelings that they take to be real love. So they have an understanding that in time they'll get married. Engagement and eventually marriage then are theirs to work through together.

Actually the process of becoming more and more involved with each other is not as smooth as it may seem. Many questions and problems can arise to delay or to hasten the eventual marriage. These questions are so universally perplexing that they must be answered one way or another by every dating young person.

TOO YOUNG TO MARRY?

Young people today are getting married in larger numbers and at earlier ages than they used to in this country. Half of all girls in America are married by their twentieth birthday. They marry boys who are little more than two years older than they are. At the turn of the century their own grandfathers did not marry until they were well into their twenty-seventh year. Nowadays many young fellows marry while they're still in school, before they have completed their military service, and quite frequently before they're ready to settle down in a full-time job.

With so many young people of both sexes entering marriage so soon, the question of the wisdom of early marriage needs airing. National figures tell us that the teen-age marriage is the least stable of all. Persons who marry before they are into their twenties more often break up than do those in any other age group.

One reason for the failure of so many young marriages is that it is usually the most impulsive, least responsible fringe of youth that rushes into early marriage—exactly those who have little chance of success in it. Another reason for the failure of young marriages is that quite a lot of them are "shot-gun weddings" which took place because a girl became pregnant. Such a marriage is notoriously poor, for obvious reasons. The over-all reason for the failure of the too early marriage is that marriage is not child's play. Two persons have to be mature enough to be ready to settle down. They must be grown-up enough to be able to assume the responsibilities and to enjoy the privileges of being married.

Just the Right Age

Studies indicate that the best age for marriage is somewhere in the early or middle twenties. When the man is twenty-three or a little more, he has completed all or most of his education, he probably is out of service, he usually is ready to get married, and he's able to support a family. By the time a young woman is twenty-two or twenty-three, for instance, she's out of school and may have had some work experience. Members of both sexes in their twenties are presumably more mature than they were in their teens. As young adults old enough to have had their share of dating around, they're now usually ready to settle down.

Chronological age is not the only or even the best measure of maturity—that certainly is true. Some teen-agers are quite mature for their age, just as many adults are immature for their years. But generally speaking, a girl of sixteen or seventeen is not grown-up enough to be really ready for marriage, any more than a lad not yet out of his teens is ready for the responsibilities of being head of the house.

How Parents See It

Most parents disapprove of early marriages. They usually prefer their sons and daughters to be very sure they are ready for marriage before rushing into it. With few exceptions, parents have an interest in seeing their children find themselves as persons before getting married. A father wants his son to finish his training and get established before taking on a wife and the responsibilities of marriage. A mother who has realized the benefits of education, whether she herself had one or not, wants her daughter to finish school before becoming a wife and mother. Parents have a considerable investment in their children. They have spent thousands of dollars in bringing up each child. They have invested much of themselves in rearing their children. So it's to be expected that they don't want their children to jeopardize their futures by marrying too soon.

Mothers and fathers know, from experience, that infatuations pass, and that impetuous love affairs should have the test of time before the young lovers rush into marriage. They are therefore apt to oppose an impulsive marriage undertaken before the couple really know each other or realize what they're getting into.

Some very young people rush into early marriage as a way of rebelling against their parents. A girl who doesn't see eye to eye with her mother may plunge into a premature marriage as her way of showing Mom that she won't be bossed any more. A fellow who is trying to declare his independence from his father may get married as a way of getting out from under his father's control. Needless to say, such drastic declarations of independence are poor bases for marriage.

Often it is the parents who pay the bills in their child's marriage. When a young couple rush into marriage before they can support themselves, they usually count upon their parents to keep them financially afloat. Parents who grew up in a day when such things were not done may not be patient with their "needy" married children. A young husband may resent having to take help from his parents-in-law. His ego may sting under the realization that he's not maintaining his own household. Difficulties come, too, when one set of parents does more for the young pair than the other side of the family. In-law problems flourish on just such feelings of jealousy, rivalry, and dependency, as many a young couple has regretfully learned.

Parental approval is an asset, and disapproval by parents is a liability in the young marriage. There appear to be two reasons for these findings. One, if the parents object because they feel marriage at that particular time is unwise, there may be some basis for their objection which is borne out later when trouble starts in the young marriage. Two, when parents approve a match they expect it to succeed, and they do all they can to help it work out well. On the other hand, if parents disapprove, they look for trouble and may go out of their way to find flaws in the marriage with sniping and goading. Such things cannot be laughed off or treated as unimportant. How parents feel is important—too important to be ignored.

GETTING MARRIED WHILE STILL IN SCHOOL

Until World War II few schools and colleges permitted their students to marry. If a young person did marry before completing his education, he was expected to drop out of school. In recent years there has been an increasing tendency for young people to marry and continue their education. How well these marriages work out is a frequent question.

Studies of married students on college and university campuses since World War II indicate that the married man is a good student. He averages higher grades, on the whole, than does the unmarried student. He feels settled as a married man, and so he wastes less time playing around. His goals after marriage are clear and highly motivated. Now he wants to hurry up and finish his training so he can get to work.

And, as a married student, he has the constant help and assistance of his wife.

Putting Hubby Through

Many a young wife of a college student laughingly says that she is getting her Ph.T. (Putting Hubby Through). By that she means that she is working to help her husband finish his education. She may help him study for examinations,

type his papers, do library work for him, or even get a job to support them both until that time when he is through school and can take over the breadwinning.

If the girl has completed her own educational plans, this is fine. But, more often, student wives drop their own schooling to help their husbands complete theirs. They often plan to go back to school after their husbands have graduated, and some of them do. But too often a girl gets caught up in homemaking, child bearing and rearing, so that she never gets back to school. She may be sorry later on when she finds herself less able to keep up with her contemporaries' cultural background—or even her husband's.

Some men don't like to be dependent upon their wives for support and make the situation difficult. Then there are men who are perfectly willing for their wives to work but who assume little responsibility around the house, so that the girl has two jobs on her hands. She may become irritable with fatigue from working under pressure all the time. If she resents having to give up her own education for such a thankless double-duty role, she may not be a pleasant wife and companion.

In School Together

There are young married couples who continue their schooling simultaneously. They get an apartment in the student housing on the campus, or they live with or near one set of their parents, and both remain students. In some situations this works out very well. In others, there are problems.

The most urgent of these problems is money. Where will it come from? Two can live as cheaply as one—but only for half as long. Somehow young married students must find money to live on while they complete their education. Veteran benefits have been a source of financial aid in recent years. Parents, in some cases, are willing and able to continue the help they were giving their son and daughter before they were married. Sometimes the couple can float a loan or live on an inheritance. Often one or both of them carry part-time work.

Problems of juggling marriage, education, and work come largely from the pressure of competing responsibilities. It takes time and attention to establish a marriage. Study requires concentration. Almost any job takes something out of a person. Some young people can take the triple responsibility; others find it just too much.

Babies Complicate Things

Many a married couple plan on finishing their education, only to find that a baby is on the way. When a baby comes, a young mother has to drop out of school. The young father may have to get a job in order to take on the additional responsibility. He may have to curtail his educational plans. When a couple marries, babies are a part of the picture. Recent studies of married university students indicate that most of them did not plan on having their babies so soon, and if they had it all to do over again they would have postponed their weddings.

Sometimes, of course, the reason why a young couple married while still in school was because a baby was already on the way. Such weddings put pressure on both the young woman and the young man to hurry up and "make things right" before the baby was born or, if possible, before the pregnancy was discovered. Most people agree that this is not the best start for marriage.

High School Student Marriages

Many people oppose marriage of high school students, even though they may approve of college marriages. They feel that college students have more of a chance. For one thing, housing for married couples is provided on many a college and university campus. Secondly, college students are older and more mature than high school students, more ready for marriage.

Many high schools openly oppose student marriages, and when students marry they are not encouraged to return to school. If they do continue on as married students they may find themselves excluded from certain student functions. Some high schools have more permissive policies about student marriages and allow such students to continue on in school after they're married. But even the most liberal high schools find it hard to approve of the marriages of their students.

Objections to student marriages in high schools are several. First is the recognition that by marrying while still in school, students are curtailing their own futures. Experience indicates that few of the married girls finish school. They drop out to have their babies or to get jobs before they graduate. Fellows who marry while still in school often drop out before they have reached their desired educational goals. The pressures of supporting a wife and family are too great to keep the average boy in school very long.

Adults in the community fear the effect of married students upon other pupils in high school. They don't want to risk the kind of talk and behavior that they feel sure will start when married students mingle freely with single ones. Whether these fears are well-founded or not is beside the point. The fact is that many adults are anxious that inexperienced young people not be inducted too soon into the more sophisticated behavior of married students.

Some teachers feel that generally it is the more impulsive, irresponsible young people who marry young. Therefore they, too, are usually opposed to early marriages. So the tendency is for high schools generally to frown upon student marriages and often to rule against them.

WHEN HE'S OFF TO THE SERVICE

Most young fellows face the probability of military service and the question arises: Is it best to marry before a boy goes into service, while he is in, or after he is through service?

The answer seems to depend primarily upon how ready for

marriage the couple is. If they are ready before he is to go into service, they may have enough feeling of unity to weather the months and miles of separation they face when he's in service. Even then they face the questions of where the young wife will live while her husband is in service, whether she will try to follow him as long as she can, or whether she will take a job to see her through, financially and emotionally, while he's away.

Marrying while a fellow is in service means a short honeymoon and little time to be together before he has to return to duty. But it may give a couple a sense of having things settled, and the security of being married might be worth the strain of separation.

Waiting until a fellow has finished his military service makes sense to some couples; they prefer to postpone marriage until they can live together. They face the strain of separation during their engagement, as well as the possibility that one or both of them may change during the interval of separation and cause their relationship to break up. But if they are well matched and mature enough to take such stresses, they may conquer them and be glad they waited before going on into marriage.

There is no one answer to whether it's best to marry before, during, or after a man has finished his military service. With each way there are compensations and complications. What any one couple decides depends upon what their relationship means to them and what they want to do about it.

SUCCESS IN MARRIAGE

The great American belief is that if two people love each other enough they will get married and live happily ever after. But it doesn't always work that smoothly. Many marriages end in divorce, separation, or annulment rather than with the bliss the couple anticipated. Our country has too high a divorce rate to give young people any basis for believing that they will get by "doin' what comes naturally." Building a marriage that lasts and brings happiness through the years is an achievement that does not come by accident. Intensive studies have been made to find out just who makes a successful marriage. Some of the findings of research and clinical studies are summarized briefly below.

It Takes Good People

Enduring, happy marriages are made by persons who have learned how to live a good life. They are conventional, trustworthy people who inspire confidence. They are usually active in religious life.

When you realize that in marriage you share all that you have and all that you are with your marriage partner, you realize how important it is that he be the kind of person you can trust. The adventurer, the irresponsible infantile person, the brittle sophisticate, may be exciting for an hour or an evening, but for the long pull of marriage someone more sturdy is needed. So it's not surprising to find in study after study that it is good people who make good marriages.

It Takes Well-adjusted People

Any marriage requires considerable adjustment on the part of both the husband and the wife. The person who has learned how to adjust to others in a variety of situations before marriage therefore makes a better marriage partner, and finds greater happiness in marriage than does the person who cannot get along with others.

One study finds that those who have belonged to organizations and have had friends of both sexes before marriage make better marriages than do those who have had little social experience. Another investigation reports that those with a minimum of neurotic tendencies are more successful in their marriages.

It Takes Happy People

The indications are that those who get married and live happily ever after are usually those people who were happy before they married. Happiness runs in families, as do divorces. In a happy home a youngster learns the habits that make for happiness. These he brings with him into his own marriage. This doesn't mean that the child of an unhappy home is doomed to unhappiness. But it does imply that the unhappiness of his childhood home may be a handicap that he will have to overcome—like any other.

It Takes Determination

Persons of both sexes who are determined to make their marriage work are more frequently successful than are those who are not willing to assume the responsibility for building it.

Larry is a good illustration. He signed up for a course in marriage at his college. These are the reasons he gave:

> You see, my Susy and I have two strikes against us in our marriage. Her parents were divorced when she was in high school. My parents still live together, but in a state of cold war in which neither one can stand the other. My father brings out all the worst in my mother; and she nags at him until he is his most unpleasant self when he's with her. Susy and I don't want to do that to each other. We want to find out what it takes to live together in peace and happiness.

Larry may or may not have found the answer to his question in his college course. But the attitude he is taking toward his girl, toward his marriage, toward his parents' home, shows the kind of honest, responsible determination to improve that makes for success.

GETTING READY FOR MARRIAGE

We have already seen that marriage is not child's play and that it takes real maturity to make a good marriage. Such maturity is not in age alone, but is in terms of how emotionally grown-up you are. If you still childishly expect to have everything your own way, you are not grown-up enough for marriage. If you get angry too easily, jealous too insanely, or resentful when your rights are threatened, you have some growing up to do before you're ready for marriage. If you still run back to your parents in infantile dependence whenever you're hurt or have to make a decision, you may need to learn how to govern yourself before you make a good marriage partner. Until you have learned to love and to accept love in mature ways, you will not find much warmth in marriage. When you enjoy responsibility, and can carry your own weight and a little bit more, you are also ready to enjoy marriage. Until then, marriage—for you—would be risky.

So it goes. Emotional maturity is a personal achievement that comes from continued development as an individual. When two relatively mature persons marry they continue to develop and to help each other grow. Their marriage then becomes a joy and a blessing to them both.

Just feeling in the mood to get married is not enough of a reason to do it. Even being in love is not enough. Many people love each other and yet would be poorly matched in marriage. Love comes not once but many times in the life of a fellow or a girl. All through the teen years members of both sexes fall into and out of love. Only when they both love and are also willing to assume responsibility for a lifetime of living together should they prepare ahead for marriage.

Getting to Know Each Other

Before two people marry they should get to know each other well. The time will come when they can anticipate each other's feelings and wishes. As they become really well acquainted, they find that they can finish each other's sentences and feel what the other is feeling even without words. They learn to communicate with each other freely and fully, with-

out fear or restraint, in ways that give a good basis for working out their life together.

In some sense, every marriage is a mixed marriage. No two people come from exactly the same background. Every couple must learn to live with these differences, whatever they may be. If a fellow comes from one religious faith and his wife from another, they have a gulf to bridge until each can get through to the other with understanding. If he comes from one economic level and she from another, if they are of different nationalities or have different ethnic backgrounds, there will be strangenesses between them. Just the fact that he is a man and she is a woman means that they may have certain psychological differences which the couple will have to meet. Working such things out takes time and effort, and mutual concern and affection.

Preparing for Marriage

Getting ready for marriage means more than just deciding when and where you will be married. It means deciding where you will live and on what. It involves discussing how you feel about children and wives working and mothers-in-law and sexual relations and going to church and what life means to you both. Any two people who approach their wedding without having given some serious thought to how they will work out their own specific personal plans for their marriage may be in for disillusionment.

Marriage involves so much over such a long period of time that it is the most demanding and exacting relationship that exists. It calls for preparation in much the same way that any other job does. You wouldn't think of applying for a job as a doctor, a teacher, or a mechanic unless you had prepared for that job and were ready to tackle it. Even more, you will want to prepare for your marriage.

That is why so many young people today take courses in courtship and marriage in schools, colleges, churches, and community programs. That is why premarital conferences— with a trusted physician, with the couple's pastor, priest, or rabbi, or with an accredited marriage counselor—have become an accepted thing. That is why books like this are written to guide those who want to think through their relationships with each other. That is why persons like yourself, giving serious consideration to all the relationships in your life, are encouraged to keep on asking questions and demanding better and better answers.

SUMMING UP

Dating leads to marriage eventually. But rushing into a precipitous marriage is foolish. It is far wiser to wait until you are mature and really ready for marriage, and to prepare for it responsibly over a period of time. One good way of readying yourself for marriage is by continuing to grow socially and emotionally in the experiences offered you by dating itself. As you make the most of your present social life, as you learn to appreciate and understand your dates and yourself, you are paving the way toward the good marriage that may be yours someday.

RESEARCH STUDIES MENTIONED OR USED AS A BASIS FOR GENERALIZATIONS ON DATING

Blood, Robert O., Jr., "Uniformities and Diversities in Campus Dating Preferences," *Marriage and Family Living,* February, 1956.

Blood, Robert O., Jr., "Romance and Premarital Intercourse—Incompatibles?" *Marriage and Family Living,* May, 1952.

Bloom, Martin, "The Money Problems of Adolescents in the Secondary Schools of Springfield, Massachusetts," Doctor of Education thesis, New York University, 1955.

Christensen, Harold T., "Dating Behavior as Evaluated by High School Students," *The American Journal of Sociology,* May, 1952.

Connor, Ruth, and Hall, Edith Flinn, "The Dating Behavior of College Freshmen and Sophomores," *Journal of Home Economics,* April, 1952.

Dubbé, Marvin C., "What Young People Can't Talk Over with Their Parents," *The National-Parent-Teacher,* October, 1957. (Report of Doctoral Study, Oregon State University.)

Duvall, Evelyn Millis, *In-Laws: Pro and Con* (New York: Association Press, 1954).

Ehrmann, Winston H., "Influence of Comparative Social Class of Companion upon Premarital Heterosexual Behavior," *Marriage and Family Living,* February, 1955.

Ellis, Albert, "A Study of Human Love Relationships," *The Journal of Genetic Psychology,* 1949.

Herman, Robert D., "The 'Going Steady' Complex: A Re-Examination," *Marriage and Family Living,* February, 1955.

Hiltner, Seward, *Sex Ethics and the Kinsey Reports* (New York: Association Press, 1953).

Hollingshead, August B., *Elmtown's Youth* (New York: John Wiley and Sons, 1949).

Kinsey, Alfred, *et al., Sexual Behavior in the Human Female* (Philadelphia: W. B. Saunders Co., 1953).

Kinsey, Alfred, *et al., Sexual Behavior in the Human Male* (Philadelphia: W. B. Saunders Co., 1948).

Kirkpatrick, Clifford, and Caplow, Theodore, "Emotional Trends in the Courtship Experience of College Students," *American Sociological Review,* October, 1945.

Kirkpatrick, Clifford, Stryker, Sheldon, and Buell, Philip, "Attitudes towards Male Sex Behavior," *American Sociological Review,* October, 1952.

Kirkpatrick, Clifford, and Kanin, Eugene, "Male Sex Aggression on a University Campus," *American Sociological Review,* February, 1957.

Koller, Marvin R., "Some Changes in Courtship Behavior in Three Generations of Ohio Women," *American Sociological Review,* June, 1951.

Lowrie, Samuel H., "Factors Involved in the Frequency of Dating," *Marriage and Family Living,* February, 1956.

Maas, Henry S., "Some Social Class Differences in the Family Systems and Groups Relations of Pre- and Early Adolescents," *Child Development,* June, 1951.

McGuire, Carson, "Conforming, Mobile and Divergent Families," *Marriage and Family Living,* May, 1952.

National Midcentury Committee for Children and Youth, "Unhappy Homes and Draft Lead Youth Problems," *Progress Bulletin,* January, 1953.

Nye, Ivan, "Adolescent-Parent Adjustment—Age, Sex, Sibling Number, Broken Homes, and Employed Mothers as Variables," *Marriage and Family Living,* November, 1952.

Nye, Ivan, "Adolescent-Parent Adjustment—Socio-Economic Level as a Variable," *American Sociological Review,* June, 1951.

Purdue Opinion Panel, *Male-Female Roles as Seen by Youth* (Lafayette: Purdue University, February, 1956), Poll No. 43.

Remmers, H. H., "Youth Attitudes toward Various Aspects of Their Lives," Purdue Opinion Panel, April, 1957.

Remmers, H. H., and Hackett, C. G., *What Are Your Problems?* (Chicago: Science Research Associates, 1951).

Stolz, Herbert R., and Stolz, Lois M., "Adolescent Problems Related to Somatic Variations," Nelson B. Henry (ed.) *The Forty-Third Yearbook, Part I, Adolescence,* of the National Society for the Study of Education (Chicago: University of Chicago Press, 1944).

Survey Research Center, *Adolescent Girls: A Nation-Wide Study of Girls between Eleven and Eighteen Years of Age* (Ann Arbor: University of Michigan, 1957).

Survey Research Center and Boy Scouts of America, *A Study of Adolescent Boys* (Ann Arbor: University of Michigan, 1955).

Wolford, Opal Powell, "How Early Background Affects Dating Behavior," *Journal of Home Economics,* November, 1948.

INDEX